T0383727

Collective Design Practices

By encouraging a critical evaluation of the contemporary processes of knowledge creation within design, *Collective Design Practices* aims to open perspectives and conversations on the immense possibilities thinking and acting collectively can have in work, education, culture, and life.

Through the observation of past and present collectives of varying scales and geographies, and reflections on the implications of dialogue, generosity, and participation in non-hierarchical structures, this concise book provides a condensed exploration of how our relationships with identity, authorship, context, and each other can shape the way we work and think together, ultimately influencing our approaches to solving the increasingly complex issues of our futures.

Bringing together reflection and critical discussion, and acknowledging the disconnection between design research and design practice, this short, accessible book provides both a point of contact to research and a point of access to practitioners interested in the possible trajectories of the extended design field.

Jaxon Pope (she/her) and **Riccardo Centazzo** (he/him), respectively Australian and Italian, are a design and research duo with focused interests in the trajectories of design education, transdisciplinary approaches to collective practices, and the constructs of identity and authorship in the extended field of design and beyond.

The two have been working together since 2014, through the formation of an independent design studio, selce studio, in 2015, and an international and transdisciplinary design collective, projektado, in 2020. Their work focuses on the intersection between design theory and practice, experimental forms of knowledge creation and sharing, and the impact that design activity has on sociocultural, political, economic, and environmental contexts. They are currently active, collaboratively, as designers and researchers at selce studio, as editors and designers within projektado collective and projektado magazine, and at Lund University, Sweden.

Collective Design Practices

Riccardo Centazzo and Jaxon Pope

Routledge
Taylor & Francis Group

LONDON AND NEW YORK

First published 2024
by Routledge
4 Park Square, Milton Park, Abingdon, Oxon OX14 4RN

and by Routledge
605 Third Avenue, New York, NY 10158

Routledge is an imprint of the Taylor & Francis Group, an informa business

British Library Cataloguing-in-Publication Data
A catalogue record for this book is available from the British Library

ISBN: 978-1-032-40812-5 (hbk)
ISBN: 978-1-032-40813-2 (pbk)
ISBN: 978-1-003-35482-6 (ebk)

DOI: 10.4324/9781003354826

Typeset in Times New Roman
by codeMantra

Contents

Preface

We will admit that we were surprised when our proposal for this book was first accepted. We felt both excited and uncertain, captured by the opportunity to bring some of our scattered thoughts finally together, yet intimidated by the prospect of doing so through a form of expression we had practised less than others.

As design practitioners who have always struggled conforming to the mainstream approaches of experiencing our own discipline, we have found infinite value in looking outside of the extended design field; in communicating through different mediums; in being part of transdisciplinary, international, and intergenerational contexts; in gaining broader and more diverse perspectives; and in putting ourselves in situations of discomfort to find alternatives to doing and learning.

Collective Design Practices is part of this shared exploration, of the journey we see many other dissatisfied designers take, and of our undying hopefulness in imagining alternative trajectories for our collective futures. Some may notice the lack of continuous and rigorous academic references and buzzwords that, maybe too often, tend to characterise written reflections and elaborations on design-related topics. This may speak, in part, of our skills, but also of our choices. We have not worked on this project to give visibility to ourselves, but to concepts that we have struggled finding, if not dispersedly fragmented, in the design literature we have consumed over the years, and that we believed were becoming increasingly important to discuss in a design field equally dispersed and fractured. This book was not written to please academic circles or to rigidly present a research of our own, but to offer an accessible point of contact for those who practise design and those who only study it.

No part of the book was singularly authored, nor do we particularly care for the two of us to ever be considered individually when discussing this work. As a duo, a couple, a collective, a community, a commune, we are ultimately one non-individual. We hope that our thoughts on this book, which reflect as much of our professional experience as of our personal one, will provoke and inspire others to question individually-centred systems and enact their own alternative processes of creation, change, translation, and communication.

We invite anyone who may want to open a dialogue on this topic to reach out to us or to others; it is often better to think together than alone.

We would like to thank Hay Futura, NullaOsta, ruangrupa, and OPAVIVARÁ! for their openness and generosity, for their curiosity in our project and the time they dedicated to it. We hope to remain in touch.

We would like to thank all of the collectives and individuals who were kind enough to show interest in the project despite not having the time to participate. We'll think of you in the future and hope to find you as busy and active.

To our friends and loved ones, thank you for your support, your excitement, and for sincerely caring for what we do, always.

For providing the ecosystem in which some of the ideas in this book matured, for representing an alternative way of thinking and learning, and for remaining a source of hope, motivation, and fun, we thank projektado and all who have come in contact with it; we look forward to our future together.

To Sheida and Naiara, we love you, and hope our thoughts in this book will express how much.

Introduction

When reading recent design-related articles, books, open calls, or research, it has become almost impossible to ignore how similarly many of their introductions begin. Phrases like 'with the increasingly complex issues designers are now expected to address' or 'as the scope of design expands in complexity' now fill, in infinite variations, the first paragraphs of much of the content that aims to offer critical reflections on the extended field of design.[1] This is so notable, in fact, that some have started to perceive these expressions similarly to how one would overused buzzwords, as banal, lazy. Yet, these sentences continue to appear, and not only in uninspired articles. Even after noticing their ubiquity, we have ourselves used similar expressions more than once, but why is that? What do they do so well that encourages their continued use?

Although there is certainly a shallower motivating component to their adoption at times, these phrases are a symptom of a widely observed issue and, perhaps, of a shared intention. One thing they do well is to frame a trajectory rather than a position, a movement towards, and with it expectations for the future. Their tone suggests the awareness of change and the willingness to imagine what could be done about it.

Design has been expanding, the death of a design discipline is the birth of two others, and as an ever-growing hydra, design has grown complex but also fragmented. The sectorisation and over-specialisation we experience relate to the ways we are conditioned to understand knowledge, to the obsession with categorisation and division, which unquestionably makes design more intricate but doesn't necessarily translate in the ability to engage in complexity.

So it is true, as those phrases say, that design has interwoven itself so critically in contemporary societies to more effectively be able to interact with systems of higher consequence, yet the question on whether it is able to do so responsibly or in a non-damaging way remains. The transition towards an extended field of design less concerned with exclusively technical or commercial issues, and more oriented towards a social, cultural, political, ecological, and economic understanding of its roles, implies the need to engage with the multi-, the inter-, the trans-, the ultra-, the extra- dimensions of practice – the need for others.

DOI: 10.4324/9781003354826-1

It only makes sense that higher complexity would require more collective approaches to design, methods that leverage fairly the diverse and plural nature of knowledge and augment our ability to learn and think together, so why do we struggle removing ourselves from the individually-centred structures that pervade our field, even after recognising their incompatibility with the future we are expecting to be a part of? Do we have the capacity to work with others in more distributed, horizontal, and open ways? These questions, and many others we will reflect upon in this book, urge us to gain broader perspectives on design and our contexts, often going beyond our immediate field of study or work, and relate instead more expansively to the way we have learnt to interact with society, with each other, with what we have been educated to need or reject, our identities, our perceived purposes. It has been difficult at times throughout this text to maintain a disciplinary focus, or to present overly specific content, we often caught ourselves discussing many issues and themes more generally, more speculatively even, rather than in their close relation to design or to its scope. We have found it impossible to be strict, almost unnatural to see things as perfectly definable, as static and separate rather than mutually informing and transforming, as individually rather than collectively focused.

Our exploration has been therefore guided by a perhaps vaguer but also broader approach, an expected consequence of delving into alternative dimensions of practice, one that favours both the consideration of complexity and the communities this complexity relates to. The aim was to establish conversations and reflections that would interest designers as much as they do educators or researchers, forming a possible point of contact between some of the fragments of our extended field and perhaps offering different perspectives on topics of wider interest and concern. So although design remains both the thematic focus and the originating framework of our contents, this book is not only addressed to designers or those who have an invested interest in design but also to those curious to rethink how to be together.

Collective Design Practices is an organised collection of shared thoughts and experiences that fundamentally questions individually-centred practices and the many systems supporting them, aiming to visibilise[2] the obscured and uncredited ways knowledge is and could be produced and shared, the role of dialogue and generosity in our interactions, and the systems through which we may think and design collectively.

By delving into diverse ways of organising and being with others, varying in scale and intention, we try to expose some of the underlying structures that actively or passively obstruct the transition towards more collective realities, reflecting on how changes in the way we understand the relationship between time, effort, and value can bring to practices that are important and destabilising. We discuss the unexpected radicality of common ways of doing, from the decentralised structure of friendship to the mindful use of dialogue as a learning and thinking process, and observe the emancipatory potential of collectives in contexts still heavily conditioned by imposed systems.

The myth of the individual genius is challenged and with it the concept of original ideas, of contributions that are considered individual and owned. The plural, varied, and composite nature of identity is explored in its reciprocal exchanges with complex contexts; we ask ourselves the meaning of a signature, of a brand, of what they show or hide. The questioning of knowledge, of where it comes from and how it can be more inclusive, allows for a reflection on design contributions, responsibilities, and accountabilities and the distribution of them in collectives and communities. We consider different ways to think of design and of those who engage in its practice knowingly or not, by taking it apart and reconfiguring it through approaches that aren't based on pervasive value systems.

The positioning of collective design practices as alternative modes of learning, thinking, and searching together allows for a deeper reflection on the educational possibilities provided by these alternatives when compared to institutional forms of schooling, and the uncertain priorities they seem to have acquired in the last decades, as academia becomes closer to the business of making knowledge profitable or is at the whims of big sponsors that condition the structuring of curricula towards commercial interests rather than the alternative paths that much of academic research likes to identify but doesn't actuate. Through a different way of understanding authorship, ownership, and responsibility, collective ecosystems represent constantly evolving and engaged learning communities, able to leverage the potential of reciprocal, relational, and composite knowledge in ways that the stricter frameworks of academia won't allow for.

Collective Design Practices is meant to be read in the order it has been presented in, as chapters tend to often refer to each other and sometimes rely on previously introduced concepts or notions. Chapter 10, 'A directory of tools and practices', is an exception to this recommendation and can be read at any time, as it aims to compile in a synthetic format a number of approaches that are discussed throughout the book and work as a sort of glossary.

Finally, we would like to remark that the content we have gathered for this book is based on our reflections, experiences, and interactions, not on indisputable truths or rules, that it is by nature limited and unfinished, a building block in the construction of a much broader and inclusive collective dialogue. We thus encourage all readers to feel free to question our content; none of it is inherently right or wrong, but it is here to make us, and 'us' includes you, think together.

Notes

1 By referring to the 'extended' field of design, we want to make explicit the inclusion of all design disciplines within our reflections. Being 'design' a word that varies greatly in interpretation in different contexts, we aim to avoid creating any confusion that may lead to the understanding of our content as oriented towards a single design discipline rather than the entire ecosystem they share.

2 The verb 'to visibilise', currently not featured in a number of prominent English dictionaries, will be used throughout this book as 'to actively make something visible'. The noun 'visibilisation' or the adjectives 'visibilising' and 'visibilised' will consequently base their use on this definition. The verb 'to invisibilise', as 'to actively make something invisible', will also be used, together with related nouns and adjectives.

References

Bonsiepe, G. and Barrett, D., 1999. *Interface: An Approach to Design.* Maastricht: Jan Van Eyck Akademie.

Catlow, R. and Rafferty, P., 2022. *Radical Friends: Decentralised Autonomous Organisations and the Arts.* England: Torque Editions.

Coyne, R. and Snodgrass, A., 1993. *Cooperation and individualism in design.* Environment and Planning B: Planning and Design, 20(2), pp.163–174.

Duman, S. and Timur, Ş., 2020. *Expanding orders of design and its implications for design education.* Online Journal of Art and Design, 8(3), pp.151–161.

Escobar, A., 2018. *Designs for the Pluriverse.* London: Duke University Press.

Illich, I., 1972. *Deschooling Society.* New York: Harper and Row.

Maldonado, T., 1995. *Che cos'è un intellettuale? Avventure e disavventure di un ruolo.* 1st ed. Milano: Feltrinelli Editore.

Maldonado, T., 1970. *Design, Nature and Revolution.* United States of America: Harper & Row, Publishers, Inc.

Whiteley, N., 1993. *Design for Society.* London: Reaktion Books.

1 Understanding design

It almost feels irresponsible, or at the very least non-critical, to start a book on a design-related topic without acknowledging, and hopefully partially explaining, some of the intricacies the term 'design' has come to carry with it. The ambiguity over the meaning of this word, and its increasingly vast application in different professional and non-professional contexts globally, has been at the centre of discussion for a number of years, mostly due to the inconsistencies and widespread confusion in its use. The issue is certainly too articulated for this introductory section to fully analyse and beyond the scope of this book to attempt in any way to resolve, but if we gingerly dip our toes into the discussion, even its surface can provide important insights and opportunities to frame this term and our use of it.

A relevant place to start, and a cardinal concept for many of the debates relating to this topic, is the idea, superficial in nature, that the more liberally a term is used, the less meaningful its intrinsic definition is. The obvious instigator of this notion being so widely understood within and beyond the world of design is the almost invasive presence of the word 'design' in hundreds of different areas of application, from the naming of entire professional fields to everyday conversations. In fact, there are so many individually defined design disciplines that even extensive research on the matter will unlikely provide a comprehensive list, with many of them supported in their separation by educational programs developed to emphasise the special nature of specialty, where study, research, thinking, and working tools are presented to each course as specifically targeted or, even worse, exclusive to that pathway. Whilst there are a number of educational programs that are moving towards a more transdisciplinary and transversal way of thinking and learning about design, the rate at which we see these programs appear internationally pales in comparison to that of novel, specific, and divisive design pathways in education.

To add to the complexity of this issue, we are now not only seeing 'design' associated with increasingly diverse terms to form or try to refer to new disciplines or approaches, but we are even starting to see contention over some of the associated terms that different professions decide to pair with

DOI: 10.4324/9781003354826-2

'design', a recent example being the word 'product'.[1] And that is not all; even longer-standing disciplines such as industrial design are often discussed in completely discordant terms, from those who see it as a companion to engineering to those who teach it as a form of self-expression and style.

This over-specialised field, plagued by the obsession to categorise and give names to even the smallest variations of an often-shared practice, is one of fragmentation, of the focus on the outcome and not the process, of demarking activities on the basis of which software needs to be used rather than what approaches, methodologies, motivations, and responsibilities are associated to them. Even those who reject the sectorisation of design practices struggle to situate themselves in this extended professional field, as they are frequently expected to be labelled and describe themselves in two-word job titles or in lists of tangible (and preferably lucrative) achievements.

Perhaps the phobia of unlabelled practices (or at least of practices that aren't labelled in relation to specific technical skills, outcomes, or market niches) is also what brought about the discrediting of many multi-disciplinarily involved practitioners as 'jacks of all trades, masters of none', a popular yet imprecise way of saying that speaks to the issue we have been introducing in the present chapter.

There is a great distinction between those who aimlessly or unwillingly change interests and occupations and those who are actively trying to bridge and connect disciplines in a process of knowledge creation that is too complex to be reduced to a single field of research or practice. It needs to be remarked that many of the disciplines existing today started from a process of questioning previously restrictive labels and the formation of alternative, and at times new, ways to understand and affect culture. This is a process that could not happen as effectively or meaningfully without a transversal and mutual contamination of established disciplines.

Over time, the word 'design' has linguistically inserted itself in varying contexts inconsistently. While in the English language it has retained some of its original applications, in other contexts this word was introduced to refer to at times very specific activities, therefore transcending the use of it, for example as a verb, that it still holds in the English language. So, while in some situations the phrase 'I'm a designer' may be easily followed by the question 'Of what?', in others this phrase would imply a specific category of design, often connected to how the word came to be known or popularised in the first place. But as the world grows more connected and globalised, these contextual understandings become challenged and sometimes endangered by the globalisation of ways to interpret and define design terminology, often in a recurrent process of colonisation in which local understanding becomes questioned or replaced by the latest English iteration of that subject. The loss in this process is one of perspective, sensibility, knowledge, culture, and approach.

Even after an initial look into the problematics of the word 'design', of definition, confusion, and ambiguity, it comes to no surprise that to many contemporary designers it has become a challenge to define themselves. Questions such as 'Do you feel like you are represented by one of the many design disciplines? And if so, is your understanding of that discipline the same as those who you work with or work for? Has this understanding changed over the course of your life? Has it changed just for you or also in the contexts around you? Are you represented by a definition of it that is now lost in the past? Or one that you can only see in the future?' are now commonplace among designers.

And although, as we will explore, defining oneself through these lines of thought may not be the most appropriate way to frame designers today, for many the heavy conditioning of contemporary societies is enough to become convinced that a quest for a technical definition of their practice is necessary to create more explicit meaning for that activity.

In our past we have ourselves discussed this issue of definition extensively, since the very beginning of our design studies, with colleagues, friends, educators, professionals, and non-professionals, and for a time we believed, as many do or are conditioned to, that the crux of the uncertainties we felt for design was in its lack of clarity, of definitions, of guidelines, which often led to debates of an excessively technical or even linguistic nature. The question of 'why design?' too often collapsed onto that of 'what is design?', while, as we later understood, maybe the why is precisely the what.

It is partly true that over the years the word 'design' has stretched so thin and wide to have lost body, significance, as once suggested by Maldonado (2010). But the all-encompassing nature of this term is as problematic as it is revealing of things to come, of the position of the myriad of disciplines it represents in our futures, in our perception of their roles, and in their relation to each other.

Has this ambiguity reached a scale in which it can't be contested anymore through fragmented definitions and must be more universally recognised in its transversal complexity? Does this give opportunities to consider design's meaning and scope under a different, more transdisciplinary, light? What many have tried to continuously define on the basis of technical knowledge, commercial scope, or linguistic variations may instead need to be defined through a different set of parameters which are less divisive and can more accurately encompass the complex reality of design today.

This concept is far from being a new revelation and can, in fact, be found in several examples scattered across design's history,[2] but even though the discourse is active (and increasingly so), it still struggles to permeate the extended field of design in ways capable of drastically affecting its economy. We are experiencing the occasional translation of some of these ideas to practice, but overall, when we look at the design field as a whole, with the countless disciplines it now encompasses, it is clear that this discourse often remains relegated to theory, critique, and academia.

Academic research in design and design practice are two parallel approaches to the understanding of this field that do not readily meet. It is not uncommon to be presented with design research written by those who don't practise design but observe it, or with practitioners who rarely produce or publish research that falls within its 'traditional' boundaries and is therefore actively or passively discredited by academia, creating a difficulty in communication and interfacing between the two groups.

On the one hand, part of the problem can be attributed to educational systems and frameworks that fail to keep pace with the accelerated growth of design practice, and that struggle to actively implement changes based on research, in some cases creating learning environments that become less relevant, and occasionally so lost in time, that they still re-present and represent the problematic and Eurocentric educational legacy of design's past, that a growing amount of young students feel rightfully disconnected from.

On the other hand, another part of the problem is, as mentioned above, one of communication between practitioners and academics, one related to the practices of sharing knowledge. In fact, the availability of new knowledge coming from both groups is not what seems to be the problem with practitioners not connecting to contemporary academic research; it's also not a problem of interest, as we are seeing an increasing number of practitioners more interested in the understanding of their role in relation to our future contexts. Instead, it appears that the problem may be one of accessibility and perceived relevance to practice.

In conversations we have had over the past years with educators, designers, and researchers, the reality of design students and design practitioners struggling to approach the outputs of contemporary academic design research was often understood as an issue of a language shaped around the writing traditions of fields that have little to do with design, of an approach too often disconnected from the experience of practice, of exclusivity and elitism typical of academic circles stuck in self-referential feedback loops, and of lack of implementation and translation of concepts into the fabric of design economy and education.

Nevertheless, even considering the divide, and at times incompatibility, that exists between academia and practice, scholarly research continues to hold great power in the realm of knowledge creation and dissemination by the virtue of being considered the 'academic' representation of design research, which, as a result, risks to position 'non-academic' research as a less formal or credible source of knowledge, as well as pushing such research away from the funding that institutional academic research benefits from and unwillingly shares.

As our brief overview of the state of design increases in complexity and begins to portray an accurately vague reality, it may be useful to take a step back from analysing some of the numerous problems entangled within it and instead start decoding and questioning the need for said issues and confusion. Is design's role in our societies so important to warrant such complexity and ambiguity?

To answer this question, we will start by explaining how the word 'design' will be used throughout the rest of this book. We have already expressed our uncertainty in providing definitions that are too rigid or technical, but we can't provide one that won't cover the most problematic sides of this field and its past, as that will be counterproductive and certainly too easy of a way out.

What was once noted by A. Gramsci (1971) in his reflections on the figure of the intellectual can also be applied to the figure of the designer, as we believe to be true that everyone is a designer but not all have in society the function of designer. Or, we could also say, that everyone designs but not everyone is a 'designer'.

Design is therefore here discussed as an ability we all have, that of connecting thoughts/ideas with effects/outcomes, that of understanding causes and consequences, that of reflecting on applications and implications. In a very succinct and simple expression we could say that design is the act of planning and implementing change (with 'and' not meaning 'or' or 'and/or', but 'and') – changes in the way we move, communicate, store our food, organise our spaces, use resources, create policies, share knowledge, consume, learn, work, eat, live, kill.

Within this interpretative framework we aren't suggesting that continuous change is inherently good or necessary, in the same way we aren't suggesting that design activity necessarily is either, but simply that this is what design has come to generally presuppose. With this in mind, there are obvious associated implications in positioning design as the act of planning and implementing change, one of them being its motives. Certainly, motivations for change can vary greatly and sit in an exceptionally wide spectrum of political, economic, social, legal, ecological, cultural, and ethical considerations, but it is precisely because of the inevitable association between change and these considerations that design cannot be discussed outside of its intrinsic responsibilities.

With the rapid and accelerating expansion of the extended design field, which is unlikely to slow in our near future, and the aforementioned increasing complexity of the projects designers are called to participate in, the scale of change that designers can today be involved in making is substantial. This increase in scope doesn't only directly affect the scale of the responsibilities associated with design practice but is also pushing the field to willingly or unwillingly accept the necessity for more collective efforts, as the degree of complexity presented by these projects becomes impossible to handle through a univocal or individually-centred approach.

The developing interest in new generations of students and practitioners to re-establish design as a more responsible and self-aware practice, one that is more socially and ecologically sustainable, ties to the need for alternative ways to perceive, define, educate, listen, work, collaborate, act, and care in the extended design field. Needs that won't be able to be discussed, problematised, or acted upon through an individual path but through one that leverages transversal approaches and their intrinsic plural nature.

Notes

1 The term 'product design', which was used for decades in connection to the design and production of physical objects/products (in part overlapping with industrial design), has concurrently been adopted in recent years for the design of more digitally oriented outcomes (in part overlapping with UX). The continued use of the term for both purposes has created considerable confusion in the job market of both disciplines, and it represents an important issue of content searchability and discoverability for practitioners, researchers, or students of these disciplines, who are hindered by search engines and directories that often fail to appropriately categorise or separate the two.
2 Examples include Duman and Timur (2020), Escobar (2018), Maldonado (1995), Manzini (2015), and Ockerse (2012).

References

Bonsiepe, G. and Barrett, D., 1999. *Interface: An Approach to Design.* Maastricht: Jan Van Eyck Akademie.

Buckley, C. and Violeau, J.-L., 2011. *Utopie: Texts and Projects, 1967–1978.* Los Angeles, CA: Semiotext(e).

Duman, S. and Timur, Ş., 2020. *Expanding orders of design and its implications for design education.* Online Journal of Art and Design, 8(3), pp.151–161.

Escobar, A., 2018. *Designs for the Pluriverse.* London: Duke University Press.

Gramsci, A., 1971. *Selections from Prison Notebooks.* Translated by G. Nowell-Smith and Q. Hoare. London: Lawrence and Wishart.

Illich, I., 1972. *Deschooling Society.* New York: Harper and Row.

Maldonado, T., 1970. *Design, Nature and Revolution.* United States of America: Harper & Row, Publishers, Inc.

Maldonado, T., 1995. *Che cos'è un intellettuale? Avventure e disavventure di un ruolo.* 1st ed. Milano: Feltrinelli Editore.

Maldonado, T. and Obrist, H.U., 2010. *Arte e Artefatti.* Milano: Feltrinelli.

Manzini, E., 2015. *Design, When Everybody Designs: An Introduction to Design for Social Innovation.* Cambridge, MA; London: MIT Press.

Ockerse, T., 2012. *Learn from the Core Design from the Core.* Visible Language, 46, pp.80–93.

Van Helvert, M., 2019. *The Responsible Object: A History of Design Ideology for the Future.* Amsterdam: Valiz.

Whiteley, N., 1993. *Design for Society.* London: Reaktion Books.

2 Beyond individually-centred practices

There are numerous approaches to working together that can be observed throughout the past and present of design as an extended field, with a few that have reached a status similar to that of a distinct design category rather than only an attitude or methodology. In fact, design activity almost universally requires interaction with other people, interactions that are formed around a series of varied systems, structures, methods, and ideals. Of the many possible ways to design with others we have decided to provide further reflections to an approach that, although neither new nor necessarily rare, is not as often represented or as widely understood as others.

When we refer to collective design practices, as we do, for example, in the title of this book, we do so referring to design practices that use the structure and approach of the collective to both organise themselves and actively participate in design activity. Our intention with this book is not to attempt to propose a new nomenclature for a typology of design or to offer a strict definition of this phenomenon but to explore it in its relation to design's current and possible future trajectories. We have no interest in establishing buzzwords or in turning an established idea into a commercial strategy, like it has been done with terms like 'design thinking'; we instead hope to put forward our reflections on a topic that we believe has more to say to designers than it currently is given space to.

Following our brief and more general introduction to design, we will try here to position collective design practices within a panorama of other well-known and practised forms of organisation, exchange, and work, not yet with the intention of providing in-depth reflections on them but instead to situate them within and compare them with other common systems, from individually-centred ones to more shared and distributed ones. There are reasons for us to talk about individually-centred practices rather than individual practices, and, in part, this relates to the aforementioned impossibility of design activity outside of welcomed or unwelcomed forms of interactions. For although independent studios with a sole designer may author their work individually and physically enact some of their processes alone, they are inevitably situated within a network of other designers, professionals, users, researchers, processes, and outcomes, and,

DOI: 10.4324/9781003354826-3

more importantly, a cultural and social domain that influence all their output. We will more extensively explore these concepts in later chapters, in their relation to influence, contributions, authorship, ownership, and identity, but it is important to clarify from an earlier point that we don't find the opposition between individual and collective to be as contextually relevant in design as that of individually-centred and collective, and that individually-centred is in no way separate to the idea of working together, it simply tends to leverage it differently and through different motivations.

Individually-centred practices are more frequently found within hierarchical systems, themselves constituting the vast majority of working structures in design and beyond. The design consultancies/companies/studios/brands of medium to large size are often good examples of this common format, which can be easily observed in almost any context and at any scale. In these environments, the disconnection between the motivations of the individual and those of the company is more evident, as designers tend to rarely have any direct say in the establishment of their employer's vision or identity and work in a more task-oriented or project-oriented way, generally in what can be seen as more technical or skill-specific roles. Their motivations remain therefore more often anchored to a personal dimension and can vary greatly in scope, going from the simple interest in having a remunerated job in the field of their choosing, to gaining experience that will help them take different responsibilities or roles in the future, to having their name associated with an influential brand to gain professional credibility, or to working alongside someone who can educate them in new skills. In the likely case that some of these motivations may be aligned between several designers in the same workplace, it is also important to remark that being situated in a community of other designers with similar individually-focused motivations doesn't necessarily form collectively shared ones – that being compatible isn't being collective. This is not to cast a categorically negative aura around these practices, or to say that they are intrinsically unpleasant or suffered through, but to assert that their potential is inevitably limited by the dimension they exist within, a scope that to some may be satisfactory, and to others less so.

Although the motivations of those within such structures are more likely to be individual, and despite the nature of these situations affecting greatly how and why people relate to each other, forms of exchange remain necessary and common. Collaboration and cooperation are two of the most referenced and acknowledged types of interaction in design, formal or informal agreements that are not always univocally understood in their function or linguistic use but are overwhelmingly present in most types of practices. Through our experience we have learnt to recognise some level of distinction between the two, based on the aims and outcomes associated with these exchanges, which may be interesting to discuss as we form a body of notions to later compare the idea of collective to.

To start, the two methods have more in common than not, an overlap facilitated by their unspecificity and by their general purpose. In fact, in both cases those involved don't need to necessarily have a shared aim beyond the creation of a mutually beneficial exchange to initiate one of these processes, nor do they need to operate through any predefined set of guidelines or rules that universally define them. They are malleable, flexible, general. One element that more notably distinguishes the two, particularly so in design, is instead the relation participants have with the output of said exchange, if there is one. Collaboration more commonly implies the willingness to have a shared outcome, the perceived or factual sharing of authorship over something. This could result, for example, in a set of products designed through the collaboration of a company and a known designer, or a software developed by two normally independent studios. The outcomes in these cases will generally be associated with all involved, and the interaction will be perceived as more sporadic than habitual, project based. Cooperation instead relates less to the need for anything to be co-created, the outcomes of those involved in this scenario remain more often separate, possibly facilitated by the exchange itself but not shared in authorship or ownership, representing a trade of services more than working together on something.

The non-essential presence of a common vision between participants doesn't obstruct some design approaches to make it their focus, leveraging collaboration and cooperation in diverse and more informed ways. When the idea of flattening a vertical structure becomes a priority for example, we see a movement towards methods of working that attempt to be more inclusive, distributed, and shared. This is true within collective systems, which rely on a horizontal structure, as we will describe later in further detail, but can also be partly observed in approaches that sit between hierarchical structures and non-hierarchical ones. One fundamental branch of design methodology that fits in this category positions the involvement of outside actors or 'non-designers', the audience that designers are intending to facilitate, at the centre of the design process. Here, a wider range of stakeholders (users, clients, manufacturers, partners, sponsors, consumers, etc.) are given space to collaboratively develop design solutions that more effectively take into direct consideration everyone's professional and non-professional experiences and insights. Two of the most commonly used approaches in this scenario are co-design and participatory design.

Understood by some as interchangeable and by others as clearly distinct, co-design and participatory design have experienced a rise in popularity in the last few decades, as they have become more ubiquitous concepts throughout most design disciplines and beyond. The core idea that connects the two is the consideration of users[1] as experts of their experience, as valuable participants in the design process, and of design as an intrinsic human activity not exclusive to professionals– in short, the recognition of users as active participants in the design and decision-making process. Through these approaches, designers often take on the role of facilitators, moderators, educators, consultants, or support, contributing to and maintaining frameworks that present non-designers with more opportunities and tools to increase their awareness of how to play a constructive part in the designing of a service, space, product that they themselves can use and benefit from, empowering voices that are often left unheard or not listened to.

The two approaches present some differences, or at least to us they do. Participatory design prioritises the inclusion of everyone throughout the process, not only through simple consultation and dialogue but also through more shared decision-making processes. Participants become in many cases the driving force of the project, yet their role remains often distinct from that of the designer. Co-design instead places more emphasis on the sharing of the act of designing as understood in a more professional sense, with additional time spent to develop a common design language between participants and designers, making the role of the designers as 'educators' or 'communicators' often more prominent and that of participants more directly related to design activity. Overall, in both cases, the question on who should have final say in design decisions is meant to include considerably the participants.

With the increased popularity and use of these approaches, it has also become easier to see both the varying outcomes they can lead to and the changes in the way some designers have started to perceive and use them. Most notably, and also quite problematically, to many designers this has become a simple way to advertise a project under a more socially sustainable light and force themselves into narratives they may not belong to. The essence of the frequent misuse of the terms 'co-design' or 'participatory design' is the quite liberal interpretation of what 'participation' means or should mean when discussing these practices. The distribution of power, or, more simply, the extent to which participants are actually allowed to participate, is a key point of instability in this extended issue of interpretation. Consultation can often become confused with participation, so even in projects that involve sensibly selected groups of users, and although numerous and relevant voices are listened to during the design process, less authority or influence is given to them. This is a crucial problem, as it is important to remark that consultation is not participation or co-design, it is data collection or research at best. Asking to a selected group insights or feedback that are then used at the discretion of the designers to continue developing a project is not what defines these approaches, differently to what you would assume by observing the myriad of projects that have come to leverage the hype associated with these terms. With designers that struggle to share or abandon control of final decisional power, the worrying tendency to lean too much into the narrative of the participants being the ones who are 'given the opportunity' to design, and exclusive and filtering processes of project maintenance and establishment, ultimately the issue that persists in the uninformed uses of these approaches is that the designers continue to design for users rather than truly with them.

Participatory design and co-design remain, nevertheless, highly relevant and valuable approaches when undertaken with appropriate accountability and responsibility on the side of the designers. The risk of them derailing into tokenistic practices does exist, as it does with most methods that can grant a positive connotation to design activity (as we have experienced with the excessive misuse of the term 'sustainability' for example), but they continue to be worth pursuing both in practice and through the exceptionally active narratives and critical dialogues that have been formed around them over the years. Collective design practices occupy perhaps slightly less space in design discourse than the above approaches currently do, but it is worth noting that discussions on collectives have been trans-contextually growing in recent years, touching the field of art perhaps a little more than other creative fields but overall showing that the theoretical interest in this subject is expanding and increasing in complexity and importance.

There are a number of factors that can be observed to help position collective design practices within this varied ecosystem and to more easily compare them with the briefly introduced approaches above: their aims, structure, longevity, and authorship systems. Collective design practices are non-hierarchical structures based on the acknowledgement of shared ideals or aims that are determined and transformed over time by the open and equal participation of all members to a reciprocal exchange of knowledge and experience. They are often oriented towards providing long-term alternative spaces for learning and doing, and establishing communities of action and reflection. Many form a more shared and distributed relation with identity and authorship, which is often solidified by the prioritisation of sociocultural, political, ecological, and pedagogical interests over commercial ones and results in outputs that aim to equally represent all who were involved and the collectively built dimension they share.

The movement towards more horizontal organisational and decision-making structures we have briefly explored in relation to participatory design and co-design remains, although amplified, in collective design practices, where the complete departure from the dispersed presence of asymmetric motivations within the group is supported by an environment which equally distributes responsibilities and roles. By doing away with fixed static positions, non-interchangeable teams, or any forms of division/filtering/exclusion, collectives maintain a more diverse, inclusive, and adaptable relational network, which is not only important for the organisational aspects of practice but especially for what it means for the preservation of balanced power dynamics within groups, something that can't be taken for granted when applying other approaches.

How equally, but also for how long, those working together are able to make their voice heard and valued across all aspects of practice is also a question that can expose additional boundaries between approaches. Collective design practices tend to be more oriented towards a lasting commitment to working together; this is quite an important distinctive feature, as a few of the ones we have introduced, including collaboration, participatory design, and co-design, are more commonly understood in relation to a project and therefore a timeframe that is expected to come to a conclusion. This can at times limit the continued inclusion of participants through the decision of specific groups to consider a project concluded and doesn't as easily allow for the dynamic transformation of a practice as the group evolves through experiences together. It is certainly harder to feel a powerful sense of commitment to a shared ideal, when the dissolution of the group is a deadline away. Also worth noting is that collective design practices represent both an approach and a structure, while collaboration, cooperation, participatory design, and co-design are more often seen as approaches, methodologies, or tools that may, or may not, affect the structure of the design practice in the long term or past the project in which they are used, making them more easily and diversely applicable. This means that a direct comparison is not always appropriate as, for example, we have seen many collectives leveraging participatory or co-design processes within their own practice.

A relevant parallel can be found in the concept of friendship, especially when evaluated as a form of organisation. Similarly to collective design practices, friendship is one of the few modes of interaction between individuals that requires a large investment of time, effort, and commitment, without necessarily resulting in a commercial or monetary exchange based on such investment (Catlow and Rafferty, 2022). There is something important about the non-commercial nature of human activity in the context of an overwhelmingly commercial global reality, and it can be easy to forget the radical position these activities occupy in our lives. In the case of friendship, this radicality is additionally amplified by the decentralised character of this social structure, one that escapes formalisation, censorship, legislation, and most forms of institutional control or categorisation. The long-term potential of it, the non-hierarchical and often dialogical decision-making and power structure, its informality, and the dynamically and collectively established goals of the relationship are all characteristic elements of collective practices that many find difficult to imagine in a professional setting yet may be experienced everyday through friendships. Friendship therefore offers a partial but compelling proof of concept for the establishment of collective realities and a strong theoretical base to re-evaluate our practices.

While collective design practices, from what we have said thus far, may appear more structured than other approaches that can conform more easily to various types of systems, it is important to not confuse rules with values. Collective design practices are more actively regulated by a set of values than other approaches are, with a sense of structure that tends to come from cohesive ideals rather than bureaucracy or strict standards. So while collective practices imply the adoption of a specifically non-hierarchical system and more distributed decision-making processes, this is not a rigid framework but operates organically. They remain on many levels informal relations, which, on the one hand, offer flexibility and potentially independence from more conventional forms of influence but, on the other hand, may remain fragile and unpredictable. Collectives may be as turbulent as friendships, with high and low points, close and distant moments, and ultimately no real contract that regulates their continuation or conclusion.

Collectives therefore require effort, commitment, generosity, solidarity, care, and time. They are ecosystems that can nurture resilient and profound bonds and result in the most impactful outputs, but they are hard work. There is the ever-present risk of clashing personalities, imbalances of power, misalignment of visions, and moments of uncertainty and crisis, but there are also more opportunities to confront issues and friction. When everyone is heard equally and every one opinion can affect the group, tension is a natural part of the process and needs to be embraced for what it can provide. In collectives, issues are more easily manifested and made explicit; there is a proactive attitude towards avoiding the simple hiding of conflict and instead fostering an atmosphere of openness and trust, where individuals understand that disagreements will bring a change not only to one side of the argument but most of the time to all. Diversity remains one of the most powerful tools of collectives as learning communities and equips them with a transversal intelligence more compatible with complex design efforts.

So far in this chapter we have attempted to provide an initial understanding of our interpretation and positioning of collective design practices, some of their basic traits and peculiarities, and a general notion of the use we will make of this concept, aiming to avoid confusion later on. The description provided to this point is therefore only preliminary and will be built upon through reflections, examples, and observation as we continue our exploration in much further depth in the coming chapters. We must also acknowledge that the word 'collective' can also vary greatly in its application. In most cases these uses don't necessarily interfere with our reflections and can actually be necessary to their comprehension, but there are other instances where it is not so. One relevant example of a common structure that we have seen several times referred to as collective, but that fits outside of the understanding provided in this book, is characterised by a group of designers sharing a studio space or other resources but working mostly independently. Certainly the formation of such communities is valuable for those involved, and it can bring great benefits through mutual support and reciprocal exchanges, but they fall more in the definition of cooperation provided above rather than of collective design practice, lacking a shared output, identity, and set of values.

Of the many approaches to working with others in design, some are more defined and understood than others, with many overlapping in one way or another. These definitions and approaches develop and expand as their meanings transform alongside the role of design and the designer within society and cannot be taken as absolute. So although for the purposes of common interpretation of our content we have attempted to frame our use of the concepts we are analysing, we wish not to draw harsh lines around ideas that impede the evolution or skewing of meaning into new contextually relevant understandings for future uses and appropriation.

Note

1 In this section we will use for simplicity the word 'users' to refer to all who have or maintain some relation with design outputs. This includes those interacting passively or actively with a designed space, service, or product and those being affected directly or indirectly by it.

References

Borgonuovo, V. and Franceschini, S. eds., 2015. *Global Tools 1973–1975*. SALT/ Garanti Kültür AŞ.

Buckley, C. and Violeau, J.-L., 2011. *Utopie: Texts and Projects, 1967–1978*. Los Angeles, CA: Semiotext(e).

Catlow, R. and Rafferty, P., 2022. *Radical Friends: Decentralised Autonomous Organisations and the Arts*. England: Torque Editions.

Coyne, R. and Snodgrass, A., 1993. *Cooperation and individualism in design*. Environment and Planning B: Planning and Design, 20(2), pp.163–174.

Cramer, F. and Wesseling, J., 2022. *Making Matters: A Vocabulary for Collective Arts*. Amsterdam: Valiz.

Escobar, A., 2018. *Designs for the Pluriverse*. London: Duke University Press.

Jenlink, P.M. and Banathy, B.H., 2008. *Dialogue as a Collective Means of Design Conversation*. New York: Springer.

Maldonado, T., 1970. *Design, Nature and Revolution*. United States of America: Harper & Row, Publishers, Inc.

Manzini, E., 2015. *Design, When Everybody Designs: An Introduction to Design for Social Innovation*. Cambridge, MA; London: MIT Press.

Ockerse, T., 2012. *Learn from the Core Design from the Core*. Visible Language, 46, pp.80–93.

Sennett, R., 2013. *Together: The Rituals, Pleasures and Politics of Cooperation*. London: Penguin Books.

Vaughan, L. and Edquist, H., 2012. *Design Collective: An Approach to Practice*. Cambridge Scholars Publishing.

3 A small design collective

projektado

Although the theorisation and more abstract reflection on collective design practices can certainly provide considerable space for both understanding and formulating notions on alternative approaches to sharing, thinking, acting, and designing, with the following chapters we intend to associate concrete examples of collectives to these ideas, with the hope to prevent some of the concepts discussed in this book from falling into the categorisation of utopian theories and be instead considered for their applied potential.[1]

The following two chapters will present two examples of currently active design collectives, with one of their main points of difference being their scale. Scale is crucial when it comes to understanding the structure, organisation, and practices of groups and is a factor that can be as much of an organic consequence as a very deliberate choice. By offering insights into the inner workings of projektado, a collective of four members, and Hay Futura of approximately 60 members, we will explore both how scale affects production of outcomes, interpersonal dynamics, identity, decision-making, crisis situations, project management, and communication, and how different approaches and contexts for collective design practices can inspire the formation of alternative realities.

projektado is a transdisciplinary and international design collective composed of designers and researchers originating from four different continents and with varied professional backgrounds and practices in industrial design, product design, urban design, and architecture. Their output focuses on communication and knowledge sharing and on the critical discussion of their industries through diverse perspectives and mediums, so far resulting in digital platforms, curated multimedia publications, interactive narratives, written articles, illustrated stories, podcasts, video and audio pieces, street poster art, web development, and other forms of knowledge creation and dissemination.

Originally initiated as part of a shared master's thesis project of two members with the aim of creating a politically engaged design magazine, the transformation of the project from a printed publication to a collective came through very early in the formation of projektado. In August 2020 a widening of a social network, from childhood friends to university peers, brought

DOI: 10.4324/9781003354826-4

together seven members from Australia, Brazil, Chile, Iran, Italy, and Spain, some of whom had never met before. The lack of familiarity with one another, the differing disciplines of specialisation, the dispersed locations of the members, and the non-commercial and unpaid nature of the project may seem like a strange combination of elements with which to establish a group that ultimately needs to operate on trust, on the awareness of each other's values and motivations, and on the belief that all can be represented by each other. So why did they come together?

For a start, the members shared a situation. Most were experienced designers, with some having had their own practices and others having worked on varied projects, but they all were about to conclude or just concluded their master's degrees and had done so within the context of the COVID-19 pandemic. They all had experienced the lack of spontaneous social connections that the physical presence at university environments usually affords and understood the radical potential that collective efforts represented in a moment of greater isolation. They also shared the belief that design needed to be questioned, that the responsibilities of their professions had to be discussed, and that a transdisciplinary approach was necessary to imagine alternative trajectories for the extended design field. Finally, they all shared at least one person they could trust, meaning that although not all members really knew each other, there was still a thread that connected all of them through established and trusted bonds. This last element is particularly interesting when considering different approaches to forming collectives, which can seem like an unrealistic task for those who don't sit within a pre-established group of equally motivated peers and friends. The example of projektado shows one possible way to initiate the sharing of something with those that you don't know, the establishment of a single chain of relationships in which each link is at least connected to another and no section of the chain is broken off from the rest.

The formation of the approach and ideals that the collective embodies was a pivotal moment in the solidification of the group, with the co-writing of the manifesto between seven people taking almost four months and resulting in just over 300 words, as everyone learned the differences and similarities between their scales of practices and the urgent issues surrounding them. The intricacies of language and the translation of certain concepts were ever-present factors, with multiple understandings of the same terminology to be dissected, discussed, and re-built together. To projektado's members it was these dialogues that proved most valuable, the process rather than the outcome. For the collective the result remains non-static, intentionally not finalised, understanding the co-creation of a manifesto as a situation through which to form or renew a shared understanding of the collective rather than one in which to establish dogmas.

Alongside this process, the collective began to define their identity, their approach to authorship and ownership, and generally the ways they would present themselves and their output. In opposition to the pervasive individualism and competitiveness of social and professional contexts, projektado decided to adopt individual anonymity as a political tool and emphasise a shared dimension by prioritising the use of the collective signature in their produced content, communications, and projects. It is worth noting however, that their approach to individual anonymity doesn't imply complete secrecy. The members don't deny their involvement in the collective and don't obscure their faces if they need to interact with external guests or participate in initiatives; their interest doesn't revolve around untrackability or invisibility, but instead individual anonymity becomes evident through a collective dimension that sees their output always as a manifestation of their shared context, regardless of the level of involvement any member had in it. The idea is that by interfacing with projektado's material, individuals shouldn't be able to be recognised or separated.

Individual anonymity and the exclusive use of a collective name is a powerful statement in contemporary society but also one that can obscure what should be visible if not approached critically and responsibly. projektado doesn't hide the diversity of their opinions or outputs behind a uniformed title, they instead embrace the value of conflict, of discussion, of disagreement when it contributes to a shared dialogue and ultimately to a shared goal. An example of this is through the use of the collective signature in pieces worked on predominantly by only a part of the collective or even a single individual. This is quite apparent in some of their work and results in contrasting styles, different languages, and varied perspectives. The way projektado maintains this possibility is through a process that involves frequent dialogue with the entire group and starts with the collective's decision to confirm the interest in the piece. Interest in this case is based on the alignment between the topics proposed and the overall trajectory the collective is currently positioned on, which generally is based on macro topics rather than specific opinions or positions. The piece is then produced by whoever decided to participate in it, and it is assessed and commented on by the other members of the collective, not with the intention of homogenising it with the rest of the collective's content but to provide a supporting and creative space for dialogue. It is in this dialogical space that the contribution of each individual becomes inseparable, even when it is the style of one person to appear more explicitly in the output, which in this way also becomes shared. Members tend to be less protective of the use of their collective name when they acknowledge the importance of diversity and plurality in going towards a collectively established trajectory.

The recurring themes of restriction and limitation that were so acute in the early stages of projektado, present in their recent educational experiences, in their physical interactions, and in their resources, are characteristics that seemingly have shaped over time the collective's approach to the output that they now produce and look to produce. Although their manifesto already problematised the divisive tendencies of the design industry, promoting instead a more mindful entanglement of theory and practice, as well as transdisciplinary, intergenerational, and international approaches, it is also in their actions that we can observe a continuous questioning of perceived or imposed restrictions. Their active experiences often aim to create situations that bring together differing disciplines, languages, modes of communication, creative processes, mediums, media, opinions, and contexts, and have done so through collaborations with a range of multi-disciplinary professionals, researchers, and students from biology, film-making, writing, teaching, designing, entrepreneurship, performance art, and more.

The predominantly virtual dimension of life under the pandemic pushed otherwise physical exchanges towards online ones, facilitating the extension of the collective's network to many contributors and collaborators that may have not been able to participate if it wasn't for the drastically different routine that COVID-19 imposed on most. The increasingly common presence of initiatives and collectives that exist mostly within a digital realm reflects both future challenges and opportunities. In the case of projektado, these dichotomies are not difficult to observe even in their moderately short history, with their virtual nature on the one hand facilitating an international group to effectively collaborate on minimal resources, form extensive collaborative networks, produce and share work, and offer alternative ways to co-learn and, on the other hand, restricting the organic forming of friendships and spontaneous interactions that are more easily cultivated in physical environments.

Although it is entirely possible to develop long-lasting and meaningful relationships solely online, with both individuals and communities managing to do so effectively through social media, forums, servers, threads, and channels, it is also undeniable that online and offline interactions are fundamentally different and differently experienced. As many can now attest to following the last few years of primarily digital communication, the organic creation of impromptu situations online can be exceptionally challenging due to the lack of sensorial stimulation physical spaces provide outside of planned encounters, making the sustenance of longer-term virtual relationships and friendships not a simple contextual consequence but a conscious and deliberate effort. Here it is also worth noting that in the case of projektado two members are, and have been since the founding of the collective, a couple. This brings to a disparity in the way spontaneous moments can occur between members, with the couple being able to discuss at almost any time, whilst most other interactions within the group remain in part restricted by the forms of communication adopted: Discord servers, emails, shared online documents.

One method projektado began to employ to allow for a more spontaneous and intimate flow of thoughts outside of allocated meeting times, and a way to help interpersonal bonds to deepen, was to create a diary in the form of an online shared document, where members would write or draw anonymous entries in moments of reflection. The framing of this stream of consciousness as a shared diary sets a vulnerable tone, allowing for more personal thoughts to be expressed and to be read. Even collectives who regularly meet physically may find this approach useful, helping to lower any social barriers that come with face-to-face confrontation, and also allowing for individuals to reflect and process information at different speeds, offering an outlet that lets realisations or thoughts that did not occur in a previous moment to be expressed using a range of mediums and styles.

Despite the horizontal structure of projektado remaining stable throughout their experience, with members' participation based on availability and decision-making through inclusive collective dialogues, circumstances did change – not only within the collective but also significantly within the lives of the members, bringing to considerable shifts in commitment, expectations, priorities, and a few times in the coming and going of new and past members. The framing of collectives as an organisational structure based on values of generosity, solidarity, care, and friendship makes the exit process of members perhaps more emotionally taxing. Whether or not the departure was amicable, the rupture of social cohesion creates opportunities for re-evaluation in structure, in values, and through the bonding that occurs when discussing the main reasons for a departure. For one member of projektado, the gradual misalignment with the collective's goals and important changes in their personal life made gaining a monetary profit from the time invested in projektado more and more of a priority, a sentiment that the rest of the members did not share as strongly and that ultimately led to their decision to leave the collective. Although in many ways distressing, the conversations that accompanied this process served to solidify other members in their opinion on working together on a non-commercial basis as a stronger form of radical action, also contributing to a shift towards differing goals for the collective overall, a revision that had not really occurred since the original finalising of the manifesto two years earlier.

The question of profit in the context of collective practices is one that easily creates tension, and justifiably so, with each individual's differing needs, availability, priorities to consider, and the changing nature of these factors over time. Furthermore, the anti-capitalist nature of collectives like projektado doesn't make them by default independent from the systems they sit within, which, for the most part, tend to have been developed legally, politically, and socially to support individuals or companies rather than collectives, vertical structures rather than horizontal ones. In these scenarios it can be notoriously difficult to legally officialise a collective practice without compromising on its structure or values, yet it remains a necessary step to be able to have access to much of the funding these initiatives would benefit from, an issue that can be exacerbated by an internationally dispersed group such as projektado, which remains to this day independent from any legal officialisation. What could be considered instability, but that would be more accurately defined as a simply more mutable system, ensures that effort needs to be a part of the equation if the group is to stay together. There are no contracts to keep people in a static position or to prevent anyone from leaving, but instead cohesion is based on trust, affection, sharing, commitment. projektado's conscious and expressed awareness of the generous nature of their reciprocal exchanges further solidifies the concept of friendship as one close to that of collectives, driven by an approach that transcends exclusively professional applications and informs more socially sustainable ways of doing and being – an approach that is nevertheless undeniably challenging to maintain over time.

In a way, the early years that are buoyed up by enthusiasm and perhaps some idealism, although fundamental, represent less the true potential of a collective practice, for it is experience, a re-adjustment of expectations, the durability of relationships through disappointment and fulfilment, and a re-evaluation of the value of time, which can reveal the true role it can play in an individual's life, and society at large, economically, socially, emotionally, and intellectually.

Taking some of the discussed aspects of projektado and reflecting on them through the scale that they embody, it is easy to see how a smaller group offers opportunities but also imposes limitations. Communication is generally more efficient, decision-making processes have the possibility to be smoother and faster, and processes of co-authoring can feel more intensively collaborative, with multiple members, if not everyone, consistently offering ideas, drafts, and iterations and actively getting their hands into all projects and initiatives the collective becomes involved with. projektado employs a consensus-based approach to decision-making whenever possible, with most decisions being preceded by dialogues that allows for all members to voice their opinions, ensuring that no one remains excluded or dissatisfied. This often means avoiding the typical design practice of butting one idea against the other until one results victorious and instead goes towards building something shared on the acknowledgement of difference, discrepancy, and diversity. This is certainly easier said than done, with differing personality types and group dynamics affecting the process greatly and, at times, the over- and under-exercised voicing of individual opinions destabilising the delicate power dynamics of horizontal groups. Although it may seem more convenient to agree in certain circumstances, a consequence of the lack of dissent is the lack of a wider variety of input, of different thoughts and opinions to add to a fertile pool of new ideas, and a danger of homogenising in approach and settling into habits that continuously lead to similar places. This requires a conscious effort to avoid, finding different ways to add new bursts of input, for example through short collaborations, as projektado has undertaken through differently themed explorations, or guest discussions, adding different voices to the collective meetings.

Note

1 Although theories labelled as utopian can more often be misunderstood or underestimated, pushing them at the margin of the extended field of design. Utopian thinking and speculative research are powerful tools of learning and creating. None of our content is meant to discredit these approaches or discourage people to try them, quite the opposite, yet we have decided to adopt a more direct and less

abstract approach to recording our reflections for this book, so as to inspire action and provide examples and insights that don't need as much interpretation or elaboration to feel applicable now.

References

Catlow, R. and Rafferty, P., 2022. *Radical Friends: Decentralised Autonomous Organisations and the Arts.* England: Torque Editions.

Cramer, F. and Wesseling, J., 2022. *Making Matters: A Vocabulary for Collective Arts.* Amsterdam: Valiz.

Deseriis, M., 2015. *Improper Names: Collective Pseudonyms from the Luddites to Anonymous.* Minneapolis; London: University Of Minnesota Press.

Jenlink, P.M. and Banathy, B.H., 2008. *Dialogue as a Collective Means of Design Conversation.* New York: Springer.

projektado collective, 2020. *manifesto,* Available at: https://projektado.com/manifesto/ (Accessed: October 10, 2022).

projektado collective, 2021, May. *Issue 1: Anonymity in Design,* Available at: https://projektado.com/issue-1-editorial/ (Accessed: December 02, 2022).

projektado collective, 2022. *Beyond Individual Knowledge Creation,* ArtEZ Platform for Research Interventions of the Arts. Available at: https://apria.artez.nl/beyond-individual-knowledge-creation/ (Accessed: December 31, 2022).

Vaughan, L. and Edquist, H., 2012. *Design Collective: An Approach to Practice.* Cambridge Scholars Publishing.

4   A large design collective

Hay Futura

When compared to most collectives we have looked into and discussed with, both those present in this book and many others in the extended field of design, scale is certainly one of the defining characteristics of Hay Futura. With approximately 60 active members at the time this book was written, Hay Futura represents a break from the more typically sized four- to ten-person design collective and offers important insights into the establishment of structures that leverage scale through its political, professional, social, and communicative potential.

Hay Futura is an interdisciplinary and intergenerational design collective based in Argentina. They came together in September 2019, first as a WhatsApp group that swelled to 150 members, at a time in which the rights to legal, free, and safe abortion in their country were in active discussion and a need for political participation was strong and evident. Hay Futura has been positioned since its inception within a political dimension, with the aim of creating a network of reflection and action capable of questioning and re-imagining design through a gender perspective and reflecting on their experience of women workers in this discipline.

By adopting the use of the word 'colectiva' rather than 'colectivo' (and therefore a clearly feminine use of the Spanish word) to define themselves, Hay Futura continuously remarks their critique of the patriarchal culture that has shaped their realities through inequalities, injustice, and violence towards women. This choice goes beyond a linguistic statement and further ingrains this group as part of the socio-political space constituted by the extended Latin American feminist movement.

Putting aside the matter of scale briefly, it is also important to notice how Hay Futura in its foundation presents clear similarities with both the example of projektado we have included in the previous chapter and with most design collectives we have explored through our research for this book. A recurring fundamental aspect of cohesion for many of these collectives can be found in the reliance on values and motivations that transcend strict disciplinary boundaries and the implementation of a more extended, transversal, and politicised view of reality. Design is therefore not necessarily a primary

DOI: 10.4324/9781003354826-5

motivation but is often seen as either a context in which to imagine change and/or a medium through which change can be enacted, communicated, and discussed. The framing of design as a non-exclusive interest or focus there-fore helps collectives to renew themselves consistently within their fields and retain a radical and critical potential in their detachment and nonconformity towards mainstream narratives and practices of design. To do so congruently, many collectives, including Hay Futura and, as we have seen, projektado, establish a shared and agreed-upon series of values.

For Hay Futura their manifesto, jointly and horizontally authored, rep-resents an enduring presence in a continuously re-evaluating and evolving practice, one that helps guide their approach as they act collectively and rein-force a sense of union that can be more challenging to maintain in larger active groups. In short, the manifesto works as a stable base for a dynamic and adaptable structure, providing an organisational flexibility that is particularly important for a group as numerous and diverse as Hay Futura.

There are several implications that come with the decision to maintain a group of this scale, some more positive than others. Through our exchange with Hay Futura, it was clear that their size wasn't only an organic conse-quence of their initial formation but that it remained a conscious choice. Their scale establishes them as a critical mass in their sector, increasing their reach through a more extended network and giving their actions more visibility both in formal and informal contexts. The political relevance of numbers is pow-erfully highlighted by a network capable not only of addressing actions of higher complexity and potential impact but also, in its diversity, to constitute a resilient self-supporting system in which varying cultural, social, political, personal, and professional backgrounds can provide a higher degree of aware-ness, adaptability, and critical relevance to the collective.

Yet, a larger-scale collective is also inevitably accompanied by a more formalised structure than other smaller collectives to remain operational and avoid dispersion and confusion; the tension between horizontality and organi-sation is obviously present but is confronted and addressed with awareness and critical action within Hay Futura. So, while their structure may appear at first glance similar to that of other non-collective organisations, additional concrete steps were evidently taken to avoid conforming to more normalised hierarchical models. This is done not only through the actual operational sys-tems they base their practices on but also through a different way of under-standing the collective, one that positions it as a living design process, in continuous construction and change. The permanently changing status of Hay Futura is as much of a point of concern for its members, at times manifesting in feelings of uncertainty and instability, as it is a continuous self-regulating measure for the collective's well-being and enduring horizontality.

A relevant example we were given of their application of these processes relates to the way the collective composed and recomposed itself over time. Less than a year after their establishment, Hay Futura took the decision to open their doors to new members for a period of two months, purposely constituting the Bienvenida commission to guide this endeavour and help with the induction of those joining the collective. During this relatively short period, the group grew considerably in number, with applications initiated via invitation by active members, in an effort to maintain a sense of trust within their shared spaces. At that stage new members had no obligation to take on any particular responsibility and were instead accepted based on their alignment with Hay Futura's founding principles. Following this period of substantial influx, the collective suffered a significant leak of personal information through their internal communication channels, which forced a revision of both their structure and their forms of engagement. Hay Futura managed to reconstruct itself through simple but effective methods, which included making the participation in at least one commission compulsory for each member, a transition that resulted in the downsizing of the collective but also in closer bonds between those involved. Through the active exploration of ways to establish participation on the basis of interest and flexible availability, Hay Futura continues to work towards escaping the more commercial modes of participation normalised within capitalist systems and is managing to maintain an environment that is both coherent to their values and variable in its dynamics.

Hay Futura is currently formed by a series of transversal working groups or 'commissions' typically of 6–12 participants, each established on the basis of different needs, projects, tasks, or themes. The commissions are themselves dynamic spaces of interaction, open to the involvement of any member of the collective that expresses an interest or desire to join them, and where roles can be exchanged or reconfigured based on the trajectory that commission takes or the longevity of the commission itself. Every member may be part of several commissions at once, and no role is mandatory or permanent, with commissions being formed or dissolved based on the needs of the collective and the projects they may be involved in at any given time. This commissions-based model offers the opportunity to provide active space for participation to all members simultaneously, without imposing restrictive limitations on task distribution, which tends to instead happen organically within commissions depending on each member's availability, motivation, or interest. Within this structure, commissions communicate with each other through plenary sessions that involve the extended participation of all commissions and that form a recurring open space for discussions of a more general character, for conflict resolution, and for decision-making on questions of collective concern.

The collective works on both internally initiated projects and external proposals of varying lengths and scopes, each characterised by its own dynamics and approaches. Ideas and opportunities are normally initially discussed within the collective and are tested for interest and availability; if the decision is made to go forward, a new group or commission is started, alongside specific communication channels, so that members can begin within the smaller scale provided by the working group to more organically distribute tasks, organise, discuss, and design. A comprehensive record of each project is kept through the recording of meetings, note taking, and the use of shared platforms and documents to allow for any member of the collective to more easily remain informed and involved in the process or to access material at a later time for reference. Projects may also require support groups, composed of members who may not be involved in the direct development of the project due to availability or interest but who may instead help through, for example, the revision of written material or necessary communication with third parties.

Although there is more structure now than there was initially, Hay Futura strongly prioritises the horizontal aspect of collective practices, and therefore any ways of working that are in conflict with the enablement of motivated and active participation are rethought and adjusted, actively redesigning and revising their system in a formative process of learning through doing. This is also supported by their discursive approach to decision-making, which they enact through complex and inclusive consensus-building processes. To preserve their output as shared and collectively embraced, voting is generally avoided, and instead space is given for all voices to be heard equally, limiting the formation of underrepresented minorities typically inevitable in voting processes that isolate those who voted differently to the majority. Within Hay Futura the opposition of a single member to a collective decision is enough to justify a re-evaluation of a said decision, making their system certainly more inclusive but also slower and establishing an alternative pace to practices that must be understood in its benefits and complications by both the members of the collective and those who interact with them.

One of the interesting aspects of this consensus-building approach, especially with 60 active members, is the clear visibilisation and acceptance of conflict as a natural part of collective being. The adoption and leveraging of scale and diversity for the great benefits they can provide come with the embracing of asymmetries and differences throughout the collective process, the active transformation of conflict into conversations, and conversations into shared ways of doing.

The generous investment of time and effort necessary for this system to exist and work is a reflection of the values that characterise this form of collective exchange and the understanding the participants have of it. As it is the case with most of the design collectives we have looked into, the members of Hay Futura don't expect any economic gain from their involvement in the collective; they instead value what being part of a network means politically, socially, emotionally, intellectually, professionally, and culturally. But the reliance on systems that actively question those that are the norm in contemporary capitalist societies can also complicate how these alternative approaches are perceived and recognised by those external to them, often resulting in the question on whether this activity constitutes a profession, activism, militancy, voluntary work, or a hobby.

The need to more accurately and formally communicate the scope of collective action is often impeded by legal systems that fail to appropriately support collectives as formal entities and that can push them to either need to structurally change for the sake of bureaucracy, therefore often compromising their ideals, or abandon the pursuit of legally officialising their practice. This wouldn't be per se a problem if it only influenced a collective's image, as design collectives often tend to prefer maintaining a certain distance from formality anyway, but it becomes more crippling as forms of exchange, funding, collaboration, production, planning, and communication can be inaccessible to groups lacking a formalised legal entity. Hay Futura themselves have been struggling with this very process, which has created internal tensions as well as opportunities to reassert themselves as critical forces. The incompatibility between non-hierarchical systems and their legal contexts is an issue that they are still aiming to resolve, but that we are convinced will result in proposals of profoundly political nature.

At this moment, Hay Futura has varied ways to present themselves to others, and their approach to authorship has transformed, with the collective signature initially favoured over that of individuals. Hay Futura now decides case by case on how to communicate who is responsible for their collective actions, aiming to support personal growth for their members whilst maintaining and strengthening the collective's vision cohesively. Contributions to publications and editorial work will be displayed alongside a full list of the collective's members, with those active having their names highlighted; in the case of public speaking, the speakers themselves are named along with a description of the collective, and when authoring work through a collective voice supports their motivations best, this approach is taken.

Overall, in their rejection of the relationship that capitalism has created between time and action, Hay Futura offers a great example of how a different awareness of time, of pace, can drastically change the relationships we create with each other and our practices. Through their scale and scope, they have confirmed feminism as a vehicle to promote diversity and inclusion, capable of giving different answers to the usual and unresolved questions, and mobilise large groups of practitioners in coordinated and shared efforts.

References

Catlow, R. and Rafferty, P., 2022. *Radical Friends: Decentralised Autonomous Organisations and the Arts*. England: Torque Editions.

Cramer, F. and Wesseling, J., 2022. *Making Matters: A Vocabulary for Collective Arts*. Amsterdam: Valiz.

Escobar, A., 2018. *Designs for the Pluriverse*. London: Duke University Press.

Hay Futura, 2021, December. *Manifiesto*. Hay Futura. Available at: http://www.hayfutura.com.ar/hf/ (Accessed: November 20, 2022).

Hirsch, T., 2009. *Feature learning from activists: Lessons for designers.* Interactions, 16(3), pp.31–33.

Jenlink, P.M. and Banathy, B.H., 2008. *Dialogue as a Collective Means of Design Conversation.* New York: Springer.

Manzini, E., 2015. *Design, When Everybody Designs: An Introduction to Design for Social Innovation.* Cambridge (Mass.); London: MIT Press.

Vaughan, L. and Edquist, H., 2012. *Design Collective: An Approach to Practice.* Cambridge Scholars Publishing.

5 Collective structures outside of design

There are a number of recurring or parallel approaches that we have found to be inextricable from both the design collectives we have had space to introduce in this book and numerous others either active today or in the past. A series of ideals and attitudes that seem to feed an overarching theme: the fundamental reliance of design collectives on aims, values, and activities that in many ways permeate past disciplinary boundaries and form a much more transversal and holistic perspective of those disciplines' responsibilities, roles, and possibilities. The almost ultra-disciplinary nature of some of these collectives' motivations suggests the potential not only to easily translate some of their practices to different contexts and areas of interest outside of design but also that the opposite is equally possible. For this reason, we have decided to dedicate this chapter to the exploration of collectives that sit outside, or at the very least at the periphery, of design.

Before we venture into our reflections on the three examples we have selected, respectively from Italy, Indonesia, and Brazil, there is still a concept that, although mentioned and in many ways implied throughout the previous chapters, still needs to be more explicitly discussed both for its relation to some of the collectives we have and will present and as a way to further understand shared practices, what happens around them, and where some of them originate.

The concept of community is one that ties closely to the idea of sharing and consequently with that of collectives. This is true, on the one hand, for their similarities, which may suggest the understanding of some communities as collectives and collectives as communities, and, on the other hand, for the more extended groups of people that many collectives tend to sit within or contribute to – communities within communities. Certainly not all groups are communities, and not all communities are collectives, but oftentimes even when these concepts don't coincide, they at least overlap or relate.

'Community' is a much broader term than 'collective' and is much more frequently used. It can simply be summarised as referring to a group of individuals who share something or have something in common, like an interest, belief, attitude, idea, space, place, culture, custom, value, norm, or

DOI: 10.4324/9781003354826-6

identity, and who have an awareness of firstly being part of said community and therefore of the unifying traits that bring these individuals together; secondly of the influence that, by being part of a community, one may have on others and others may have on them; and thirdly of the implied responsibility every member has in caring for each other and for the well-being of the community itself.

At times communities seemingly appear out of thin air, a sort of spontaneous flurry of activity that brings together oftentimes strangers to enthusiastically discuss and share common interests. With increasingly globalised and interconnected societies, these communities can now more easily transcend geographical and linguistic contexts to include a multitude of voices of differing cultural, social, economic, and political backgrounds, providing fertile ground for transformation, expansion of vision, and alternatives to norms. They are sometimes in the form of a comment thread of a YouTube channel, a Discord server, a Reddit forum, or, in the physical dimension, a climbing gym, a skatepark, or a local cafe or bar. These communities share a disconnection from a necessarily commercial or professional sphere and instead sit within a dimension based on genuine commitment in participation. No one is forcing anyone to take part, the desire is innate, and the initiative comes mostly from the individuals involved. Communities are not inherently good or bad, but they are a varied and flexible form of coming together that can lead to diametrically opposed results, radical thoughts, volatile passions, and significant actions.

As some communities become more organised, with the intention to create events, relevant outputs, start a business, or just spend more time together, a structure often is developed to manage tasks, provide opportunities, and organise time. This may be very informal, especially at first, but to a certain degree a commitment is made and a social contract is established and embedded within the fabric of the community and the everyday lives of those who are part of it. This may be as small as an agreed-upon communication channel or the establishment of a decision-making process, but it is also one of the possible starting points from which a collective may form, with consciousness of it or not – an organic evolution of an interest into a passion, a passion into something shared, and something shared into a lifestyle.

As with organising any group, large or small, the hurdles are many, but when energy, hope, and enthusiasm are high, as is often the case with a new initiative or project, there is opportunity for structural foundations to be laid so that there may be more chances for a collective to remain active for longer periods of time whilst maintaining passion, fresh perspectives, and income, if it's desired. Whilst sometimes short and intensive bursts of collaboration produce incredible and important action that can act as a fast and maybe even a sort of disposable outlet for developing ideas or ways of working, it is a sustained and longer-term collective practice that offers glimpses into completely unexplored ways of living, interacting, and experiencing.

NullaOsta

The intersection between life and collective practice, context and output, is one of the common elements we can observe in the three examples featured in the present chapter, beginning with NullaOsta, a group that came together in Bologna, Italy, in 2000. Although initially formed around the production of zines on social issues, a medium focus that shifted after one year, NullaOsta represented in its years of activity an important and, in many ways, successful attempt at supporting the establishment of a stronger punk/hardcore music scene and counterculture in Bologna and in Italy, providing physical and social contexts in which their community could find important shared experiences and imagine alternative ways of being together.

The group, originally four members, but that fluctuated through their 15 years of activity between one and eight, began their story by approaching an already squatted and self-managed social centre, locally known as 'Atlantide', in search for a space to situate themselves in. Atlantide was a 'cassero', a small and almost fortress-like building built in the 19th century, located at the edge of the historical centre of Bologna and in close proximity to one of its wealthiest neighbourhoods.

When NullaOsta arrived, Atlantide had already been occupied for a couple of years and was at the time self-managed by two activist collectives: Antagonismogay (a LGBTQIA+ collective, who later started the Smaschieramenti Laboratory) and Clitoristrix (a lesbo-feminist collective). NullaOsta inserted themselves into this reality, becoming the third group to share responsibility over the use of the space, and with them brought a music scene that was based on self-production and DIY, on the push against the invisibilisation of marginal realities and the commodification of culture. The organisation of concerts acted as the peak of their collective activities and their main form of expression as a group, resulting in regular events which brought together bands from local to international, from folk to crust. The framing of it all under 'punk/hardcore' related more to an attitude or approach rather than the presence of very strict musical boundaries or limitations.

NullaOsta is probably the most spontaneously and casually managed group out of those we spoke to; their process of organisation was informal, natural, and somewhat contextually reliant on the space they occupied, which was relatively small, like the group themselves. Scale played an important part in their day-to-day activities; as a small non-hierarchical group tasks were not assigned but taken on voluntarily, and their limited number meant that everyone had to participate, or few would be left with the work of many. Members came and went, in an unfixed and spontaneous way; sometimes simply giving a hand by default of being present at Atlantide on the day of a concert was enough to become initiated. Interestingly, the only time they took in three members who had explicitly requested to join the group it didn't last long, almost like the forced nature of insertion broke the flow of Atlantide's unique ecosystem.

Although their internal dynamics were informal and unstructured, NullaOsta was able to maintain an effective organisational system with the bands they invited to play, at times on a weekly basis, ensuring all equipment needed was present, distributing flyers and posters around the city, preparing meals for them at their arrival, and finding a place for them to stay when necessary. Coordinating the use of the space with the other collectives of Atlantide was also reliant on some level of organisation, which for a time took the shape of a simple physical calendar, where groups could express their interest in using the space on a certain day, and the others would write their replies below.

The group never referred to themselves internally as a collective, in part due to the actively political connotation this term holds in Italy but also due to their proximity to other collectives that, to them, fitted more into this definition. However, it is through not only the messages that were delivered through the punk/hardcore scene but also the act of occupying a space, sustaining a non-commercial social and cultural activity for 15 years, and contributing to the formation of a reality outside of an existing and imposed way of living which inherently gives their actions political weight. They didn't have regular assemblies or meetings, an aspect that some of the members regret not creating the situation for, as, although things ran smoothly for the most part, the opportunity to imagine together what more could be done was never really manifested. It was not until the notice of a possible forced eviction by the city council that regular assemblies between the collectives of Atlantide began to take place, which, despite a few years of legal disputes and concerted collective efforts on behalf of the occupants, ultimately resulted in the permanent closure of the space, which then fell in disuse.

The last squat in Bologna's city centre, Atlantide was forcefully closed in October 2015, as riot police dragged out the non-violent occupants and bricked up the entrance. The space of Atlantide was possibly the most structured part of the group, and neither NullaOsta nor some of the members who were part of the other collectives managed to recreate the same synergy that was experienced in those years elsewhere, bringing NullaOsta to disband shortly after the eviction. This speaks to the importance of the physical dimension of communities, the spaces and places. Although the three groups self-managing Atlantide were mostly independent in their activities, the physical space they shared made their collective presence permanently and continuously visible, creating a dimension that rejected fascism, sexism, racism, violence, xenophobia, homophobia, and transphobia. During a concert organised by NullaOsta, politics were in the air even when not discussed, in the feminist slogans and art on the walls, the countless stickers, flyers, posters which told the story of a place that had become a haven for the gay, lesbian, trans, queer, feminist, and punk population, in the hand stamp one would get at the entrance of every concert, boldly stating 'SONO FROCIS-SIMA!' (I'M SUPERGAY!). This inter-mingling of ideas, ideals, and realities brought together perspectives that may not have coincided naturally, shaping a different way of experiencing punk/hardcore culture, one that profoundly confronted the macho attitude that was shaping this movement in other realities, and that brought everyone to question and reflect on their identities, to understand this space beyond music, and to value what was shared.

ruangrupa

ruangrupa is an artist collective that was formed by six friends in the year 2000 in Jakarta, Indonesia, with the intention to offer a space for the artistic interests which weren't being sufficiently supported by their local ecosystem at the time. The group consciously defined themselves as a collective, an early statement to the way that they would approach their working processes and their outcomes, and established themselves as an environment of spontaneous interactions, critical thinking, and radical doing. Twenty-two years later, ruangrupa still exists as a space, metaphorically and physically, and over time they have adjusted, tweaked, and renovated their practices and structure as they evolved as individuals and as a collective. Whilst art remains their common language, the professional backgrounds of members vary, including architecture, political science, curation, journalism, music, and more, feeding the evolution of their practice and pushing towards a trajectory that aims to be increasingly more transdisciplinary and diverse. Currently the collective is made up of ten core members, those who are involved in most major decisions and endeavours, and numerous other more casual members, who come and go without any formal initiation, often in response to the needs of active projects.

Although throughout the years ruangrupa has taken on more and more complex initiatives, they still very much function as a group of friends working together on a project. They don't have strict formally scheduled meetings but rely on their day-to-day interactions in person, on WhatsApp, or Zoom, intersecting casual and professional, to give shape to an atmosphere in which all feel personally close to everyone enough to understand their personal and collective status. This feeling of closeness, of friendship, of being able to trust each other's motivations and actions without the need for formal guidelines, is also reflected in their understanding of their collective values. In ruangrupa shared values are considered to be intrinsic to their relation and were not made explicit or written down until the need to communicate them succinctly to others came in more recent times; members had learnt to trust each other's sensibility in knowing what would be good for them and what wouldn't.

A certain degree of spontaneity also informs their distribution of roles and tasks, as members don't necessarily all take part in a project but decide based on interests or availability, they work around the inevitable shift in priorities that come with changing life circumstances, and they share a deep understanding of the strengths and weaknesses of each other, allowing them to delegate tasks and count on one another to go forward in the right direction. They tend to avoid voting in favour of a more conversational and discussion-based approach to decision-making, similar to that of other collectives featured above, and generally a recurring strategy that can be observed in many systems and structures that go towards more horizontal and flexible ways of doing. In the case of ruangrupa, their cultural context has partly shaped their predilection for dialogue and has created a space in which opinions, issues, and conflicts are not suppressed but made evident and talked through, at times resulting in frustration or inconclusive exchanges, and often in a slower pace, but that nevertheless bring meaning to their practices.

It is only with one of their latest endeavours, GUDSKUL, that they have had to formalise more of their processes, due to the complex structural nature of the project which brings three separate collectives together: ruangrupa, Serrum, and Grafis Huru Hara. GUDSKUL was formed in 2018 as an informal educational space in Indonesia that aims to simulate collective working and encourage critical dialogue through the lens of contemporary art. As a public learning space, the initiative expands on the concept of community already prevalent in ruangrupa's work, using the potential of alternative forms of education to destabilise and propose collectively. The project is still young and has somewhat been simmering in the background of the massive international curatorial endeavour that ruangrupa is at the tail end of after three years, but it continues their ongoing exploration of different modes of organising, learning, sharing control, and creating on varied scales.

This exploration was also very much part of the idea behind the quinquennial 100-day international art exhibition, documenta fifteen, that the group was given responsibility to curate for its 2022 opening in Kassel, Germany. For ruangrupa, documenta represented an opportunity not only to visibilise but also to enact alternative approaches and proposals aimed at moving the critique of the art world from theory to practice, from what is often labelled as utopian discourses to concrete attempts on a large scale. The exhibition brought to question the processes and practices of an art world too reliant on ideas of competition, individualism, and commodification of culture that in many ways echo the reality of other fields, including that of design, and instead moulded itself around a model of reciprocity and sharing based on community, collective practices, and distributed resources.

Through these ideas, ruangrupa also challenged their own role, that of curators, taking the decision to let go of traditional forms of control and to decentralise decision-making, organisational, and curatorial processes. The artists invited to exhibit at documenta fifteen, which included a large number of collectives, communities, and collaborative initiatives, became in this way active participants in co-organising the event, fostering and supporting an ecosystem in which responsibilities, roles, and resources were shared beyond the officially selected curatorial group, and a different experience of art could be brought forward. The event gave space to the less object-oriented practices, to the intersection of life and art, of informality and imposing international exhibitions, of interdisciplinarity and contamination.

The sheer vastness of the project, as well as its extended duration, inevitably invited moments of turbulence alongside moments of significant importance. The members of ruangrupa were since the very beginning split on whether to take on the responsibility for documenta, with concerns that an endeavour of such scale and mediatic exposure could endanger their well-being as a collective and even bring to a breaking point, due to the informality of their bonds and the impossibility to force things through without a compromise on their shared practice. Yet ruangrupa was ultimately able to bring forward a number of the alternative approaches they had wanted to explore through this event and contributed to an international network of conversations that are permeating not only the art world in notable ways.

As made evident by the distribution of control through documenta and by the organisational model of GUDSKUL, ruangrupa, similarly to projektado collective, Hay Futura, and OPAVIVARÁ! (as we will later introduce), places acute emphasis on the collective dimension of their co-creations, and therefore do not individually sign work. Their individual contributions, be they ideas, visions, contacts, are absorbed within the collective consciousness to be discussed, dissected, reconstructed and shared, shared as a process, shared as an outcome, and most importantly, shared as an experience. The individually motivated, career-driven approach to growth and notoriety meets high resistance and frustration in the slower, more deliberate, communal ecosystem of moving forward together.

ruangrupa don't claim to be a model for horizontal working, nor have they ever aimed to be, acknowledging the asymmetry that comes with informality, strong personalities, close friendships, and the natural interpersonal dynamics that occur in many groups. But their approach allows the members to live closer to their ideals, directing their focus away from individual gain, from a capitalistic approach to success, from a nine to five, Monday to Friday schedule, and contributing to a more relational and shared way of experiencing life, one in which if a person gets ahead, then everyone does.

Although different in many respects, ruangrupa and NullaOsta are similar in their strong relationship with physical spaces and with the communities these spaces support, grow, and organically form. They have both represented safe havens for socially and culturally engaged communities in urban contexts and points of critical and radical engagement with locality. Their extended life is also something worth reflecting upon, as both ruangrupa (with 22 years of experience and still active) and NullaOsta (with 15 years) embody meaningful and impactful initiatives that have managed to operate around flexible and informal structures for an extended period of time and that have done so without prioritising personal profit, confirming the viability of alternative collective structures.

Of course, their contexts are very different, and so are the scopes of these groups, but through our conversations with them, it was interesting to notice that some of the elements NullaOsta had recognised to have been more neglected during their time together are the same ruangrupa thought to be valuable in their protracted existence, which brings us to ask ourselves whether the ultimate dissolution of NullaOsta was not only brought about by the forceful disconnection from their spaces but also by a different approach to collective practices that made them less inclined or prepared to continue. The elements we are referring to are mostly two: a sustained active reflection on the collective itself, which some members of NullaOsta believe would have made a difference in their ability to imagine and do more collectively, and the exploration and diversification of activities, which have helped ruangrupa to remain involved with multiple realities when projects came to a conclusion and the will to act remained.

OPAVIVARÁ!

OPAVIVARÁ! is an artist collective based in Rio de Janeiro, Brazil, that focuses on the themes of sharing and exchanging and on the tension between public and private spheres through the creation of interventions and actions in urban spaces and cultural institutions. Their focus areas are addressed through their output and projects of public participation as well as through their formation and status as a collective, as an enacted statement and a means to visibilise ways to experience art as accessible, popular, shared, touched, lived, and alive. The occupation of any space open to the public, be it a permanent squat like in the case of NullaOsta or a temporary public moment in the case of OPAVIVARÁ!, is a powerful means to situate a group or collective within a larger community, one that actively shapes the contextual relevance of these shared actions and that questions through experiential practices visible and invisible social, political, and cultural boundaries.

The 'blocos de rua', improvised street parades by and for the people of Rio, remain to be their biggest inspiration, as instances of pure spontaneity, drawing passers-by with music and an innate human desire to connect, socially, emotionally, and physically. This atmosphere of pure freedom, of collectively formed experiences, of art that comes to life, serves to drive their practice and their desire to establish, or at least suggest, alternative ways of experiencing a city and the use of its shared spaces. Temporary public kitchens bringing strangers to prepare, cook, and eat food together; a performative collective pipe smoking experience; a 30-person tandem bike that navigates the city offering free rides to anyone willing to see where the bike will take them; a set of joined hammocks that sway and move with the rhythm of the interacting public; and a variety of nomadic devices, appliances, and apparatuses that stimulate the unexpected are just some of the interventions that OPAVIVARÁ! has initiated over the past 18 years together.

Active since 2005, OPAVIVARÁ! has varied in size from seven members to eventually stabilising at four for the past eight years, a scale that has allowed for their processes to feel more efficient yet has required them to remain consciously aware of the possible dangers of stagnating into a closed loop of thought and input. Transformation for a collective can be as challenging as it can be valuable; we have observed this in earlier examples, and it was once again made clear through our interactions with OPAVIVARÁ! and their reflections. Yet, the opportunities or methods necessary to initiate transformation are not always apparent, sometimes relying on an update in the structure of a group, the inclusion of different participants, a change of approach, an unexpected process, sometimes even a pause. OPAVIVARÁ! has been delving into this question and exploring it as they look at their future and at the trajectory of their shared practice.

Being this our fifth example of a collective structure, it is easy to trace parallels and form connections: horizontality, flexibility, contextual relevance, social awareness, coming to decisions through dialogue, and avoiding voting are only a few of the processes that OPAVIVARÁ! shares with other groups. Their approach to authorship also echoes that of almost all collectives we interacted with, a prioritisation of the plural and the multiple, and a rejection of individually authored works. OPAVIVARÁ! further expands their exploration of a collective identity by taking the additional step of avoiding printing, announcing, or stating the names of those involved in the collective, instead seeing their signature as a collage of shared experiences and inspirations, as a symbol of the reciprocal exchange of multiple and diverse visions that shared and participated environments offer. From romantic relationships forming to conflict stalemates that require outside mediation, the collective understands themselves as a microcosm, a small snapshot of society, with all of the tensions, joys, transformations, and biases present in daily life but within a structure in which everything can be discussed and resolved collectively, and no voice is silenced.

One point of difference that sets OPAVIVARÁ! apart from the collectives we have seen above is a more intentional and proactive approach towards generating income, an element they prioritise more than other groups who instead tend to see it as a consequence rather than a goal, or that don't consider it at all. Profit is certainly an ever-present point of contention that is echoed in many collectives, regardless of their area of interest or type of outputs. While some collectives have managed to drive a wedge between the concepts of time and money, imagining and acting on alternative paces and economies, this is not always contextually possible and certainly not easily achievable, especially in realities in which the economy of art struggles to support the artists. The fact that OPAVIVARÁ! has maintained profit as a priority for the past 18 years, albeit not always successfully translating this need into income, offers yet another glimpse into the very real and diverse possibilities that a collective way of working and living can in fact viably provide.

References

Bellinetti, G. and Rostkowska, A., 2022. *What Documenta Fifteen Offered to the Future - Documenta Fifteen Closing Days #1-* opinion, Metropolis M. Available at: https://www.metropolism.com/nl/opinion/47748_what_documenta_fifteen_offered_to_the_future_documenta_fifteen_closing_days_1 (Accessed: January 10, 2023).

Borgonuovo, V. and Franceschini, S. eds., 2015. *Global Tools 1973–1975.* SALT/Garanti Kültür AŞ.

Buckley, C. and Violeau, J.-L., 2011. *Utopie: Texts and Projects, 1967–1978.* Los Angeles, CA: Semiotext(e).

Catlow, R. and Rafferty, P., 2022. *Radical Friends: Decentralised Autonomous Organisations and the Arts.* England: Torque Editions.

Cramer, F. and Wesseling, J., 2022. *Making Matters: A Vocabulary for Collective Arts.* Amsterdam: Valiz.

Deseriis, M., 2015. *Improper Names: Collective Pseudonyms from the Luddites to Anonymous.* Minneapolis; London: University Of Minnesota Press.

Hirsch, T., 2009. *Feature learning from activists: Lessons for designers.* Interactions, 16(3), pp.31–33.

Jenlink, P.M. and Banathy, B.H., 2008. *Dialogue as a Collective Means of Design Conversation.* New York: Springer.

NullaOsta, 2021. *Atlantide: Hardcore D.I.Y. PUNX - Live 2001/2015.* Bologna: ZOOO Print and Press.

OPAVIVARÁ!, *Sobre/About.* Available at: http://opavivara.com.br/sobre--about/ (Accessed: October 12, 2022).

ruangrupa, *About.* Available at: https://ruangrupa.id/en/about/ (Accessed: November 22, 2022).

Sennett, R., 2013. *Together: The Rituals, Pleasures and Politics of Cooperation.* London: Penguin Books.

Vaughan, L. and Edquist, H., 2012. *Design Collective: An Approach to Practice.* Newcastle upon Tyne: Cambridge Scholars Publishing.

6   Identity, authorship, and ownership

As we take an additional step in forming connective lines of reflection between diverse collective practices, we can quickly, and with no difficulty, observe a number of recurring threads that transcend disciplinary contextualisation and that almost ubiquitously inform their activities. The ultra-disciplinary and entangled nature of these threads is not unusual in contemporary societies, and it is, in fact, common to many lines of discussion that affect global action and understanding, as they situate their stability in the almost inescapable structures of neoliberal and capitalist systems. The scale at which they need to be discussed and understood is therefore considerable, and although design provides a particularly relevant example for the purposes of this book and will be used as a primary reference throughout the present section, it is necessary to remark the importance in maintaining a variable scalar focus when approaching this topic.

In this chapter we explore the themes of identity, authorship, and ownership; the relationships designers have, create, or believe to have with their output; and the socio-political dimension these relationships hold. Much has been produced in relation to these topics, with many different paths of exploration contributing to their linguistic, philosophical, political, cultural, historical, and legal dimensions, although not as commonly in explicitly design-related contents. Considering the scope of our book, we will therefore abandon the improbable attempt to provide a comprehensive perspective and instead start our investigation from the more contemporary ideas that these concepts have come to represent in a global context heavily conditioned by individual exposure and recognition, by the commodification of ideas for individual benefit, and the extended commercial reality of individual identity as brand and source of income.

A good place to start may be to question why concepts of collective identity, authorship, and ownership continue to be seen as either exceptions to the norm or are simply misunderstood and mispositioned as they remain anchored to more individually focused forms of understanding. Movements, ideas, brands, companies, trends, nations are more than often associated with the faces of single individuals, faces that become familiar symbols of intricate

DOI: 10.4324/9781003354826-7

realities and oversimplified, and therefore only partial, representations of something built by complex plural exchanges. Why is this considered normal? Who and what is being invisibilised through this process?

A relevant example worth discussing, sitting outside of design, is that of the famed Nobel Prizes and how their awarding procedure shaped and mis-shaped the understanding we have of certain fields of research/work and of their history. The specific issue we are referring to here is a notoriously con-tested and controversial rule stating that a Nobel Prize can't be shared by more than three individuals, a significantly low number considering the fields of research that are in the first place eligible for these prizes (Yong, 2017). To put things into perspective, many of the research papers in chemistry or phys-ics that have announced findings that either won or have been nominated in the last decade often included author lists that spanned across multiple pages, with hundreds, if not thousands, of individual names included. Yet, with no exception, only three of those contributors would be able to share any of the benefits provided by winning a Nobel Prize: the title, the status, the money, the exposure, and the crystallisation of one's identity as the principal force and 'genius' behind it all.

This is not only an important issue of attribution and justice but also one that contributes to the establishment of a way of understanding practice as an individual's sport, as a quest for personal recognition and exposure. By creat-ing the illusion that the possibility of the individual breakthrough exists, is worth pursuing, and is a desirable outcome, these prizes risk to actively invisi-bilise the role of collective or collaborative practices which, although neces-sary in most scientific fields, can then become perceived as more competitive acts, a necessary evil to achieve individual aims. In failing to evolve from rules that create the impossibility to rightfully attribute authorship, ownership, or provenance to most, if not all, contributions that are awarded the prize, Nobel Prizes are one of many structures that continue to highlight the absurd-ity of the still deeply enrooted myth of the Romantic genius, of the individual (most likely white and male) inventor, artist, and visionary.

Organisations, institutions, universities, as well as the legislatures that structure our interactions with the concept of property often follow a simi-lar pattern, intentionally or unintentionally cultivating approaches that focus on individual achievements. So the issue is not only to be linked to those who are embracing the quest for personal recognition and success but also, and perhaps more importantly, in systems that actively and sometimes legally condition individuals to take on these quests, obstruct the consolidation of alternative views towards collective practices, and continue perpetuating a centuries-old stereo/archetype which fogs what the motivations to produce knowledge really should or could be. This last point is made particularly evi-dent in the unfortunately pervasive belief (very notable in design) that the new, the novel, the original is something to always strive for, that innova-tion is good and is so when never thought of before, and that uniqueness and independence are qualities that those who achieve notoriety in their fields embody. A belief built on these values supports individuality far more acutely than a collaborative or collective approach, building on the aforementioned 'genius' narrative and seeing the impact of an 'original' concept diluted when many voices have contributed to it.

The general domestication to embracing individual recognition as an ultimate aim of contemporary life extends beyond professional and academic spheres. The exceptional changes that globalisation, virtual communication, and social media have brought to the structure of our professional and social lives have completely reframed the concepts of private and public. In the case of identity, we have seen a multiplication of each person's identity through their interaction and engagement with increasingly ubiquitous and varied platforms. A single individual might very well appear, communicate, and behave differently on their Twitter, Instagram, Facebook, LinkedIn, or TikTok accounts; on their personal websites; with the different social/professional/ family groups they interact with in person; or in the exchanges they have through email, WhatsApp, Discord, Zoom, Skype, or Messenger. Identities are today multiple and not necessarily congruous; they are fragmented and rarely self-reliant; they are ultimately complex and not univocal. The private and the public are therefore constantly reshuffled, as the different identities of an individual are curated to be seen or unseen, known or unknown, by specific groups, a process heavily informed by the approaches to public visibility and discoverability that different platforms or contexts are structured around. In this way, whilst an identity may only have the possibility to be seen by a handful of people, another one (even curated by the same individual) may have the potential to reach thousands, creating powerful tensions between physical and virtual, and the decision on which of an individual's identities take priority over others.

The push towards more reach-oriented identities, and the possibility of economic gain through their reach, helps to both perpetuate interconnected narratives of the genius/hero/influencer/celebrity/star/artist/entrepreneur and to further develop our economic and social models on the statistically improbable pursuit of these myths, ultimately establishing a very effective form of control that, by relying heavily on virtual forms of communication and content sharing, can acquire an almost ultra-contextual status.

Design certainly doesn't escape the influence of these narratives.

From the Romantic idea of genius artist and its 'celebrity' counterpart to the active discrediting of collective practices through awards, institutions, universities, workplaces, and laws that prioritise either the individual or the company, much of what we have introduced so far finds a correspondent in design.

If we take star-designers as an example (who in different contexts or disciplines may be called celebrity designers, archistars, artistars, or else), and its contemporary successor represented by the boutique design brand, we find not only clear references to the figure of the 'artist genius' discussed above but also the effective transition towards the artist as art, the designer/brand as design, of a face or brand identity as a main source of attraction and profit. Here an identity is both sold and bought into, leveraging digital communication in increasingly sophisticated ways and adding to the other status symbols characteristic of consumerist societies something that sits between a lifestyle and a persona. As brands become the new celebrities of design, associating to recognised or influential studios becomes desirable and at times necessary for those who work within this industry, a phenomenon that is shaping newer generations of designers to understand their profession through brand guidelines rather than its potential implications.

But beyond the image these figures and structures project, and the narratives they shape, they remain reliant on at times very large groups of people both within and outside their practices. This system of authorship and ownership becomes ultimately based on public recognition and media interaction and is meant to continuously reinforce the identity of the star-designer/brand by indiscriminately absorbing and invisibilising the contributions of others. In these systems, identities are easily lost in their relation to a final output, as contributors can't have their individual identities seen but also can't feel included in any form of collective identity, as it doesn't exist.

The almost paradoxical situation that has come to be the norm in design and many other fields is that although most, if not all, design activity relies in practice on different modes of collaboration or, at the very least, interaction between groups or individuals, the nature of these interactions is still too often guided by forms of individualism. Collaboration is often seen as a compromise to personal freedoms, as competition, as a negotiation of ways of working and producing outcomes that risks to lead to unsatisfactory results for the individuals involved. This scenario develops a strange sense of personal ownership that makes people obsessively dissect outcomes for the privilege of being able to say 'this part of this idea is mine' or 'it was my idea first, but then they changed it this way'. In this atmosphere of hungry egos and defensiveness towards one's idea, everything is seen as an addition or subtraction made by an individual, an exchange based on supposedly professional experience where the dimension of collective ownership or authorship doesn't exist and where no contribution is indistinguishable from a specific individual – a group as the sum of its parts.

By identifying the individual as a clearly divisible part of the total and forming an understanding of the whole as neatly separable, we fail to provide any understanding or consideration for the collaborative processes that are in the first place forming, willingly or unwillingly, the practice of design – the space between individuals, or, even better, the space where individuals exist together. If designers lose grasp of this dimension, it will become difficult to see collaboration outside of what constitutes personal loss or gain. What could be shared ideals and motivations become instead atomised and privatised concepts, to the point that even individuals who have something to share may become competitive and uncollaborative. This disconnection from any form of shared ideal, beyond the interest in being remunerated, contributes to a working culture based on the performance and completion of tasks and aimed at growth in personal profit and status. The role of the designer is reduced to that of a technician, enclosed in bubbles in which the focus remains on the applications of technology, strategies, approaches, and methodologies rather than on their implications, with good design becoming a synonym of good business.

But how can a different perception of identity, authorship, and ownership change this approach? How can we contribute to the transition that sees the designer going from being a part of something to being part of something, from individual presence to collective participation?

Whether it is by questioning the individual, intellectual property, or profit, most examples that touch on said transition represent an inherently contestational and political force. They are radical for the simple fact that they sit outside or at the margins of the unreasonably established belief systems that contemporary Eurocentric capitalist societies support.

We can find an example of this phenomenon in the excessively negative connotation that within design is given to what is referred to as 'rip-offs' or 'copies', the unlicensed or unauthorised production of legally protected properties. In their going against the lingering legacy of design needing to be 'original', and questioning both the authorship and ownership systems that have been crystalised through the establishment of intellectual property laws and the historically western perception of the 'unoriginal' as necessarily inferior and immoral, these products[1] have contributed to the establishment of particularly interesting design ecosystems, of knowledge communities, and new forms of acknowledgement towards the origin of a product that help debunk the myth of the 'stroke of genius' and construct more accurate and just narratives on the process of knowledge creation. This shift in focus has often supported these ecosystems to become more able to effectively work together, to maintain a more distributed ownership over their output, and to prioritise collective goals over individual ones.

Another example to which we provided a number of references to in previous chapters is that of collectives that establish themselves on the basis of shared ideals and values rather than economic profit or social status. The political dimension of these groups is inherent even simply for their defiance of a mainstream vision of value but tends to generally expand beyond an exclusively implicit and passive dimension, to one that wants to be informed, conscious, and active. Within these systems we can find opportunities to reconsider the distribution and value of identity, authorship, and ownership and to do so through different scales of application.

Through collective practices we can experience a model where the designer is seen as an active member of a critical community. Within this model, knowledge, experience, and skills reside within the community, a community in which the role of individuals is reasoned and justified on the basis of its relation to other roles, and the collective experience forms the basis of all practice (Coyne and Snodgrass, 1993).

The community therefore comes to exist through the establishment of a collective identity, one based on ideals and values that are dynamically formed by variable modes of sharing. This identity represents a construct of the dialogical, emotional, and physical exchange that the members of the collective continually and reciprocally support; it is not autonomous but reflexive, as it bases its stability on the relationships people form between each other and, therefore, with a particular socio-cultural framework. So although on the surface it may seem like brand identities and collective identities present distinct overlapping aspects, with the implementation of cohesive styles or approaches, the less evident presence of individual authorship, a 'vision' associated with the identity, and a clear lifestyle associated with the 'vision' itself, it is obvious through a simple analysis and reflection that they both support and represent incompatible systems. Whilst the employees of a brand may find themselves needing to fit an imposed mould of values that is addressed to the market, the members of a collective find in their shared identity themselves and their plurality.

As much as the adoption of a collective identity or signature acts as a fundamental cohesive element in horizontal structures, the continuous confrontation with the lingering remnants of more mainstream forms of doing can make it challenging to sustain. We have heard of many instances in which collectives have used their shared signature despite the opposition of some of the members. This example shows both the invisibilising action a shared signature can potentially have, but also reveals a problem in the decision-making processes that a collective adopts. We have already discussed in previous chapters the benefits and challenges of differing decision-making models, but it is curious how most of the instances we have seen associated with this issue were dependent on a voting system. With voting and the presence of a majority, we always have a minority that through this process can be excluded from having equal influence on the decisions the collective takes. To maintain a horizontal and distributed structure, collectives would most likely benefit from taking a distance from voting, from effectively competing on what idea would be taken further, and instead go towards other forms of decision-making that, although often slower, can more effectively support the very foundation the idea of collective is based upon. Voting can remain a useful tool to quickly gauge the status of the collective but will need to be followed by other processes, such as discussion, shared deconstruction and reconstruction of ideas, and ultimately decision-making, which more often than not in the examples we have analysed is through different forms of consensus building.

The invisibilising effect of a collective signature can also bring to issues and questions of responsibility, especially in the previously mentioned cases in which internal tensions bring to differing sentiments towards the collective signature by the members. In a situation in which all members feel equally represented by the collective identity, there would be no reason to think that the responsibility wouldn't be as equally distributed, but in other cases the attribution of responsibilities over the collective output becomes more complex and unclear. Offering a general reflection or solution to the myriad of issues that may come from these situations is unlikely, but from our research it seems like once a collective signature or identity stops defining all equally, the path towards internal conflict, exclusion, imbalance in power dynamics, and the verticalisation of structures is often short and disruptive. This tells us that as much as it is important to initially form a shared awareness of a collective identity, to continuously question it and revise it is a vital task for the collective's well-being.

A feeling of equal responsibility within a collective can also work as an effective tool to keep participants engaged and attentive, as the more distributed identity is, the more likely those involved will want to know what and why is being produced under their shared name. Certainly trust and experience go a long way in these situations, and we have seen members of collectives, particularly larger ones, in time becoming less reliant on each other's approval on smaller project-based decisions, yet trust can at times become an excuse for a passive attitude towards the collective's activity, through which some may by default agree to other members' initiatives under the premises of trust, only to become less involved in projects and have less 'work' to do. Passivity is in many ways the antithesis of collective practice; it is a distinctly present influence of a world accustomed to consume itself on dreams of convenience and apathy.

As the scale of identity associated with a design output grows from individual, or a collection of individuals, to purely collective, we can expect a corresponding change in the relation the design output has with ownership and authorship, one that is more horizontally distributed, less fixed, or even nonexistent. For the majority of design workers, ownership remains as of now a volatile possibility that rarely coincides with authorship, as clients, employers, or those at the head of brands and companies one works for, mostly retaining sole control over it. Owning an idea, a design, is a concept that, although legally and socially accepted, remains deeply controversial. We will reflect on some of these aspects in the following chapter, but the very possibility of it suggests a way of thinking that sees ideas abstracted from their contexts, a problematic understanding of novelty as innovation that most times obscures both all who have directly or indirectly contributed to an idea and the pre-existing knowledge, academic or not, those ideas have been built upon. The perpetuated narrative of the 'genius that did something first' becomes visible again in these attitudes, and it is unfortunate that many of the laws which control intellectual property were developed and failed to evolve from a moment in time in which these Eurocentric Romantic myths were popularised and in which the individual was the sole entity capable of representing genius. The commodification of knowledge that mainstream systems of authorship and ownership support as the logic of property and market becomes part of our every day, rapidly leaching into our cultures to turn 'counter' into 'pop', is at odds with the transition towards identities so plural to be legally undefinable, knowledge so distributed to futilise the figure of the author, and a policy of donation and generosity that deconstructs the concept of owner and of owned. Moving towards a more collective approach to practice makes design more capable of questioning and proposing, criticising and changing, evolving and involving.

Note

1 For ease, 'products' has been used here as a macro category to refer to all products of design activity, with the scope of the aforementioned 'copies' including and not limited to physical componentry, digital interfaces, consumer goods, brand identities, colour schemes, form language, service design, production techniques and technologies, and materials.

References

Allison, D.H., 1966. *Anonymity in Design* (Doctoral dissertation, University of Iowa).

Baudrillard, J. and Benedict, J., 2005. *The System of Objects*. London: Verso.

Biagioli, M. and Galison, P., 2014. *Scientific Authorship: Credit and Intellectual Property in Science*. New York: Routledge.

Coyne, R. and Snodgrass, A., 1993. *Cooperation and individualism in design*. Environment and Planning B: Planning and Design, 20(2), pp.163–174.

Deseriis, M., 2015. *Improper Names: Collective Pseudonyms from the Luddites to Anonymous*. Minneapolis; London, University Of Minnesota Press.

Jenlink, P.M. and Banathy, B.H., 2008. *Dialogue as a Collective Means of Design Conversation*. New York: Springer.

Maldonado, T., 2005. *Memoria e Conoscenza: Sulle sorti del sapere nella prospettiva digitale*. Milano: Feltrinelli.

Maldonado, T. and Obrist, H.U., 2010. *Arte e Artefatti*. Milano: Feltrinelli.

Manzini, E., 2015. *Design, When Everybody Designs: An Introduction to Design for Social Innovation*. Cambridge, MA; London: MIT Press.

projektado collective, 2021, May. *Issue 1: Anonymity in Design*. Available at: https://projektado.com/issue-1-editorial/ (Accessed: December 02, 2022).

Vaughan, L. and Edquist, H., 2012. *Design Collective: An Approach to Practice*. Newcastle upon Tyne: Cambridge Scholars Publishing.

Yong, E., 2017. *The absurdity of the Nobel prizes in science*. The Atlantic. Atlantic Media Company. Available at: https://www.theatlantic.com/science/archive/2017/10/the-absurdity-of-the-nobel-prizes-in-science/541863/ (Accessed: December 15, 2022).

7 Context as designer

There is a fundamental principle in forensic science, attributed to the French criminologist Edmond Locard, that is summarised by the axiom 'every contact leaves a trace'. While this principle has had mostly the disciplinary-focused intent of describing the reciprocal material exchange that happens between any two items that come into contact, and the material evidence they leave behind for the investigation of a crime, we find that the most interesting side of this statement is one that considers a more open interpretation of the concept of contact. If, for example, to the material dimension of contact, mostly based on the physical collision or touching of bodies, we add an intellectual dimension, or an emotional one, or a sensorial one, or any other form of interaction, tangible or intangible, suddenly we are moving this principle from one useful to a specific field of study to one interesting in the more general understanding of human interactions, forms of collaboration, and knowledge creation. In our case, we will try to use 'every contact leaves a trace' as a simple reading lens for the relation design outcomes have with the contexts they originate from, in an attempt to once again question the more conventional concepts of authorship and originality that define contemporary design and further motivate the movement towards different, and more collective, models.

The first barrier that we find in trying to make our reflections explicit is the vagueness of the word 'context'. Putting aside the myriad of possible interpretations of this term, we will try to directly explain our use of it, to facilitate the reading of this section that in many ways relies on this understanding. When we talk about context in relation to design practice, what we refer to is the sum of environmental and human states that collide with the design practice and output we are trying to analyse, experience, and discuss. To make some examples, it may include the people who were in contact (directly or indirectly) with said practice or output, their histories, emotions, personalities, cultures, experiences, languages, relations, identities, ideas; what has been exchanged between these people, verbally, silently, emotionally, visually, physically, intellectually, culturally; the historical, geographical, environmental, cultural, political, social, and economic realities the design practice has been in contact with, for whichever amount of time; the contacts that different bodies (human,

DOI: 10.4324/9781003354826-8

non-human, or inanimate) may have had and the traces left behind; what was shared, like spaces, foods, costs, tasks, visions, ideas; and what was perceived by those entering in contact with any of these elements, in any combination they may have been experienced.

Through this interpretation, context can be understood similarly to the concept of atmosphere in its more colloquial use: an experienceable reality made up by a complex combination of more or less tangible states of being, at times difficult to define in words but nevertheless obviously present and diffused. It is what we refer to when we ask someone, for example, what the atmosphere in the room felt like during a meeting or what kind of atmosphere a restaurant has. Our definition of context also shares similarities with some more academic applications of 'atmosphere', for example in relation to G. Böhme (2018) and the debate on aesthetics, but we won't delve deeper into this possible connection, partly due to our only superficial knowledge of the current developments in some of these philosophical discourses and, in part, as we intend to relate more to the terms that are common to those practising or studying design.

Alongside these similarities, there are also important differences between the colloquial 'atmosphere' and the 'context' we refer to. While an atmosphere is generally described as something that can be subjectively experienced and perceived, context can't be accurately absorbed only through a subjective sensorial exercise and instead requires a more intricate reflective and critical process to be more clearly understood, one that is both more dialogical and less individually-centred. The reason being that context includes, as mentioned above, many aspects that are not always made explicit to our senses, and provide instead a more implicit, compounded, and sometimes hidden influence.

The influence that contexts exert on design practice is the crux of this chapter and probably revealing of our choice to associate a principle of forensic science with authorship in creative practices, moving context from something that can only be observed to an active participant in the design process, context as designer. Through this logic, the concept of authorial contribution is deeply questioned, when we understand silence to be as relevant as sound, or the layout of a room as important as a technical drawing, contributions become almost impossible to attribute and to neatly separate, they become more clearly recognised as a manifestation of a context and are diffused in what is shared. The context therefore both takes on a more expressively communicated active role in the design process and is the shared space in which the knowledge, skill, and experience of the collective reside, in constant exchange with themselves and all elements giving them shape. This forms a complex network of mutually defining relations, in which designers aren't perceived in an isolated way but through their contacts with contextual elements, bodies, states, ideas, and more – relationally.

There is often an interest, mostly based on compensation or authorial attribution, to try to quantitatively determine the contribution each person brought to a specific design project. Sometimes this is calculated on the number of hours each person spent on the project, the types of tasks they performed, who came up first with which idea, their official job title, or a combination of these factors. But very rarely we see the use of alternative, less hard data-reliant approaches to the understanding of what goes to shape a final outcome and to what extent. There is no denying that different contributors (human or not) can have dramatically different influences on what becomes the product of a design practice, but what we are trying to explore here is the deconstruction of the idea of these contributions as individually attributable. Going back to the thought of 'every contact leaves a trace', it becomes difficult to see anything as truly individual, and through this lens the concept of originality, of authorship, and of genius greatly loses traction.

In a way this perspective aims to help situate the designer and further sensibilise them to their actual importance and role, over perceived or advertised ones. In attaining a broader and more abstracted perspective on the infinite threads that relate them to the whole however, a sense of individual authorship can melt away together with a sense of purpose, evoking a humbling effect and deflation of the overall importance of the individual as well as existential questions. The sensation could be compared to the sometimes overwhelming realisation of our significance in an expanding universe, when we zoom out of our own singular reality and begin to gain glimpses of the complexity that surrounds us, the impossibly entangled network of relations, emotions, inputs, outputs, forces, contacts, ideas, and bodies existing in almost complete oblivion to each other. The designer is but one figure surrounded by very many, and when no scale of application or practice seems impactful enough, or our vision permeates in dimensions so unfamiliar and unexplored that seem impossible to grasp, how do we manage the paralysing effect these thoughts may have on our actions as designers?

The answer is not straightforward, univocal, or possible to be narrowed down to a few words but, at least in part, relates to the ways designers understand and test their perceived limits and their motivations. Through processes of exploration, of probing into adjacent spheres of research and activity, of connecting to others with different knowledge and experience, of attempting something unknown, designers can begin to form a more conscious idea of the scale at which they can act effectively and embrace the discomfort of moving past the scope they have been trained or educated to focus on. A collective ecosystem tends to promote this explorative itinerary and organically both push what individuals believe they can manage and fuel their stimulus to do so. The far-reaching scale and impact that collective action allows is not only so for the simple sum of the individuals' potentials but also for the growth of each individual's capabilities through their reciprocal exchanges in a diversely experienced context.

The repositioning of context as active designer we have introduced above, and the complete unravelling of the idea of contribution it implies, further feeds the existential questions we have been delving into and poses new ones by destabilising the designer's perceived control and moving it, or we could say distributing it, away. If the context becomes the designer, how are we now to see designers? And what comes of their role?

Their practice becomes perhaps more of a question of focus, of consciousness, an actor who is looking for certain triggers, connections, who has learned to notice. But with a more mutable, relational, and certainly nebulous position and purpose, the tension between activity and passivity, between the active context and the designer whose concentrated power we have just stripped away, intensifies, and the risk to see the figure of the designer falling into indifference and detaching itself from a perceived sense of responsibility towards their output becomes a worrying possibility. Here, once again, the axiom 'every contact leaves a trace' guides us through our reflections and helps us prevent the fundamental idea of responsibility to escape design. Following this line of thought, when there is contact (in the more open interpretation of this term provided above), be it active or passive, there is a trace, there is a contribution. This suggests that contributing is not only a choice but sometimes a non-choice; contribution is intrinsic to contact and so is accountability.

This analysis may seem more of a conceptual splurge than an applicable tool, yet we have seen through our research that similar forms of understanding to those described in this chapter often fundamentally structure the approach collectives maintain in their practices. The horizontal sharing of resources, the lack of individually authored or owned output, seeing one's contribution as a product of the environment the collective provides, alternative modes of recognising involvement, have all been recurring constants in the experience of collectives within and outside of design.

The multifaceted dimension of contribution that comes from embracing context as designer helps visibilise the invisible, represent the unrepresented, include the excluded, and depict a more inclusive and comprehensive idea of effort and involvement that is directly contrary to mainstream working practices and prevailing systems of thought. This approach offers the opportunity to form a general predisposition to design practice that more effectively responds to the trajectory we are seeing our field going towards, one that is more concerned with the contexts a design practice enters in contact with and that supports the increasing need for transdisciplinary, international, and intergenerational collaborations in these contacts. The transversality of thought implicit in this trajectory brings sharing and exchanging to the forefront and makes space for collectives to become increasingly necessary contexts for design practice to situate itself. Through this lens we can extend further the concept of context as designer to include that of collective as designer, informing the core understanding that leads to the adoption of shared identities and signatures introduced in the wider discussion on identity, authorship, and ownership of the previous chapter.

Through the various (somewhat disjointed) lines of thought we have presented so far, if we attempt to more succinctly define what the role of the designer comes to be, we are guided towards the concept of translation. Whilst to many the meaning of translation instinctively relates to written and spoken language, its notion sits within most layers of activity and cognition. Spanning from viscourse or visual conversations to emotional intelligence, translating is an action that designers tackling problems and perceiving the world around them must become accustomed to doing deliberately and effectively, to use as a powerful method of communication and practice. The relationship between knowledge and context, perception and experience, imagination and creation can be now observed, deconstructed, and critically analysed in alternative ways. The understanding and awareness of two or more contexts, and a design ability to create connections, to communicate experience and knowledge, to form the language of informal equivalence between them, become in this way descriptive not only of translating but also of designing. Through physical, digital, and conceptual means, designers translate meaning, intentions, ideas, technologies, and concerns into newly discoverable and understandable contexts, expanding the possibility for learning, dialogue, implementation, and action, towards those who didn't have direct access to it before. The initially proposed definition of design as 'the act of planning and implementing change' is added to by finding both a focus, that of the collective, and a perspective, that of translation. Translation is a powerful analogy for design, implying the need for plural and diverse knowledge and rendering ineffective the narrative of the new.

As a final thought in our dissection of the relevance, provenance, and distribution of design contributions, we question the role of established institutions, organisations, universities as primary contexts for learning and gaining knowledge, and their ability to evolve at the same speed the design disciplines' understanding of themselves does. How can we provide the ecosystems and the contexts necessary for this evolution, which for now remains too often unsupported and marginalised? How do we educate newer generations effectively in their comprehension of the intricacies of knowledge creation and sharing in their fields? If we begin to reject the assumption that it is by graduating in a design university or from interning in a studio that one becomes a designer, if we take a step away from these pervasive systems and start reimagining the core ideas behind contribution, attribution, ownership, and identity through a more shared and collective approach, we are, in a sense, left with somewhat intimidating yet exciting opportunities.

References

Böhme Gernot and Thibaud, J.-P., 2018. *The Aesthetics of Atmospheres.* London: Routledge, Taylor & Francis Group.

Bonsiepe, G. et al., 2021. *The Disobedience of Design.* London: Bloomsbury Visual Arts.

Bonsiepe, G. and Barrett, D., 1999. *Interface: An Approach to Design.* Maastricht: Jan Van Eyck Akademie.

Escobar, A., 2018. *Designs for the Pluriverse.* London: Duke University Press.

Manzini, E., 2015. *Design, When Everybody Designs: An Introduction to Design for Social Innovation.* Cambridge, MA; London, MIT Press.

Pfützner, K., 2017. *Designing for Socialist Need Industrial Design Practice in the German Democratic Republic.* New York: Routledge.

projektado collective, 2022. *Beyond Individual Knowledge Creation,* ArtEZ Platform for Research Interventions of the Arts. Available at: https://apria.artez.nl/beyond-individual-knowledge-creation/ (Accessed: December 31, 2022).

Schuppli, S., 2020. *Material Witness: Media, Forensics, Evidence.* London: MIT Press.

Shaler, R.C., 2011. *Crime Scene Forensics: A Scientific Method Approach.* Boca Raton, FL: CRC Press.

8 Design through dialogue

It may come across as one of the most obvious, almost naive, suggestions for a collective design practice; we converse all the time without thinking about it, and it is almost unavoidable in all forms of working, collective or not, why make a thing of it? Yet, it is precisely the ubiquitous nature of dialogue that renders it necessary to draw attention to, for without it, we would struggle learning anything outside of what we experience individually and directly, a narrow and oddly isolated perspective of a complex ecosystem, but with it, we may still easily fail to do the opposite.

What we would like to explore here therefore, rather than the unlikely possibility of a complete lack of dialogue in collective practices, is ways of leveraging conversation that inform positively the processes of working together. The consistent presence of a discursive approach within collectives further highlights a necessity to dissect and understand the role of dialogue within non-hierarchical groups, as a means of decision-making, conflict resolution, learning, sharing, and existing together.

Before continuing, it is worth acknowledging the differences that exist between the terms 'dialogue' and 'discussion'. One of the generally agreed-upon distinctions between the two is the intention and attitude of the participants, with dialogue representing a more explorative and open process, in which participants build on each other's ideas rather than defending their own, and discussion approached in a more confrontational manner, where ideas are compared rather than entangled. It is also necessary to clarify what means of communication we refer to through the use of these terms, which may instinctively suggest face-to-face verbal interactions, yet to us also includes a wider network of mediums and formats, such as the sharing of visual content, exchanges on online platforms, voice messages, and other physical and digital forms of communication that together inform the intricate dimension of dialogue, discussion, or conversation.

As speculated through the framing of context as designer, our relational experiences are inseparable from our thoughts and practices, and the act of conversing, with colleagues, friends, family, and strangers, is one of the many forms of exchange that can transform our understandings and create important

DOI: 10.4324/9781003354826-9

new connections. Inputs and ideas are absorbed, digested, and regurgitated with mutated meaning, intention, and perspective by the context we enter in contact with, allowing for a continuous intertwinement of knowledge and culture entirely unique to any specific moment. The presence of a sketch accidentally left on a whiteboard can play a role in a dialogue had in the same space a few hours later. A suggestion to order food whilst continuing an activity sets a more casual tone, allowing quieter participants to speak more freely and share pivotal viewpoints.

In a shared context of mutually defining inputs and outputs, intentional and participated dialogue is closest to the process of thinking together rather than that of stating. Dialogue becomes here understood as an act of collective creation as opposed to selection, in which the value of process supersedes that of single ideas, which become instead nebulised in what is shared; inhaled and exhaled by the collective in a purposeful cycle of transformation and evolution. In participating, there must be therefore an understanding that most of what goes into a conversation is deemed to change, and to do so organically. The purpose is not to maintain ideas stable whilst trying to change each other but to change together as the collective experience manifests into shared meaning and knowledge. By promoting less conditioned and more distributed ways of knowing, dialogue reinforces the collective trajectory towards less fragmented and more transversal design communities and acts as an important tool to accompany said transitions.

Similarly to what we have seen with the idea of forming a collective or questioning the concepts of identity and authorship, the thoughtful use of dialogue, although seemingly common, represents a radical approach to thinking, learning, and communicating, one not as supported by prevalent forms of understanding. To initiate a dialogue is for this reason not as easy as it may seem, for although it may not require or necessarily benefit from much preparation or structure, it still relies on the abandoning of pervasive ways of approaching co-creation and the understanding of the intrinsic value of dialogue as an educational and creative resource.

One of the most manageable formats to start exploring collective dialogue that we have used ourselves extensively is the so-called 'discussion group', a group of people who at least partly share an interest and possibly a relation (this may be an established collective or a group of friends or peers) that come together to talk. This exercise doesn't imply the use of dialogue as we have so far defined it but can certainly provide space for it, as we have both observed in our research and experienced in our practice.

The suggestion of a discussion circle or group is certainly not a novel one; in fact, our own introduction to the possibility of adopting this activity was through our coincidental participation in a close friend's small self-organised gathering at a local bar. The group we met on that occasion were researchers in various scientific fields who were coming together to discuss transversally some of the specific problems that they were individually engaged in, seeking feedback and different perspectives. Their choice of meeting place reflected and suggested specific attitudes towards their studies and interests: firstly, their need for more spontaneous and conversational spaces than academic environments were providing them 'officially', spaces that were less conditioned by specific disciplinary boundaries or academic standards; secondly, the intertwining of the social and the professional, the extension of research to the dimension of everyday life and that of friendship; and thirdly, their intellectual commitment to others beyond themselves, sharing as a way of knowing. In our dissatisfaction with our own educational ecosystem at the time,[1] we were encouraged by the self-determined and meaningful nature of the gathering, and pitched it to our peers, together planning a format that would suit our context and needs.

From there began a periodical series of themed informal conversations we named 'Design Discussions',[2] which took place in various locations, often a restaurant, pub, or someone's living room. Each session was initiated by a different person briefly presenting a design-related theme to the group, followed by an open conversation of approximately three hours in which the participants, with a semi-conscious awareness of remaining on track, would search and think together in their shared curiosity. There was rarely the pressure of having to reach a conclusion, or coming up with an actionable plan as a result of a conversation, and we believe this helped sustain the atmosphere we needed and our relationships. One of the most simple actions that was consistently adopted from the very beginning of Design Discussions, which upon reflection seems to have been instrumental in the transition from casual chat to focused dialogue, was the recording of each session. Very often our conversations weren't listened to again, but in the moment, the knowledge of being recorded added to the intentionality that open dialogue requires, the participants were more aware of themselves, so that the flow of the dialogue was maintained and was built upon in a more deliberate manner. We practised active listening, we spoke when we were sure to not interrupt, we used visual cues between each other as forms of acknowledgement, and we were pushed closer to the edge of our comfort zones whilst remaining within a non-judgemental space. In this crucial moment, we were acutely aware that we were taking control of our learning, that this activity had more significance to it than just a group of students meeting and talking, and that non-institutional collective education was both possible and often more valuable than what scholastic curricula offered to us at that time; it was empowering.

As an actionable exercise that could be readily adapted to varied practices and contexts, Design Discussions allows us to reflect on how the focused decision to participate in a collective dialogue can lead to rewarding shared experiences of knowledge creation, creativity, and emancipation from more formal or 'recognised' modes of learning. Dialogue or, as we previously framed it, collective thinking, represents an action that almost infinitely increases the potential learning power that we individually and collectively possess. A key aspect is intentionality, purpose, entering a dialogue with the conscious aim of sharing and understanding together, not only pushing a personal agenda or aiming to 'win' but committing intellectually and emotionally to something shared and not always expected, finding a space in which vulnerability is a part of being together. By temporarily putting aside what are perceived to be fixed opinions, it is possible to accept new ideas otherwise dismissed; in removing assumptions we remove the impossibility of venturing into territories normally obscured and open ourselves to absorbing and reconfiguring rather than only confronting and reacting, creating a sense of common ground that aims to stimulate inclusivity and alternative thoughts.

The considerable effort and commitment that are required to sustain a discussion group, however, especially at first, make at times for fragile ecosystems. The difficulty of participants to change their attitude towards conversations, the imbalance in power dynamics within the group, the intersection of different personalities and backgrounds, and the inconsistent level of focus between participants are all common breaking points for these activities. We will address later some of the approaches that can be adopted to alleviate tensions and manage conflict, but it is worth mentioning now, in relation to our example of Design Discussions, that three factors, beyond those already mentioned, particularly favoured the continuation of our activities and the extended cohesion of the group involved: friendship, scale, and agreement on engagement practices.

While the use of friendship as an element of stability has been previously discussed in relation to collective practices, scale is another factor that we believe facilitated the experience of Design Discussions and generally a very impactful variable in dialogue. This specific exercise worked very well with 6 people, and we have experienced it being quite effective and easily manageable in the range of 5 to 10 participants, but we have also talked with and observed other groups and collectives that have managed to establish dialogue spaces for 20 or 30 people, sometimes even more. There is no perfect group size when it comes to dialogue, or collectives for that matter, but with scaling up we can expect several consequent effects. More time needs to be dedicated to dialogue in greater numbers; this is in part to leave opportunities for all to equally participate and avoid the marginalisation of those who less readily jump into the conversation and also for the increased complexity of ideas and perspectives that a larger ecosystem embodies, which need more time to be shared, processed, and built upon. Another equally relevant change we would most likely experience in bigger dialogue groups is the more complex maintenance of a safe, horizontal, and equally motivating environment, the monitoring of power imbalances and unjust practices. Depending on the size and experience of the group, this can, at times, result in the need for (ideally rotational) roles that go beyond simple participation in dialogue and become more oriented towards facilitation, observation, supervision, and record keeping, which can more easily identify and address where and how balance is being compromised.

With 'engagement practices' what we are referring to is the ways we interact with each other, the tones, the emotions, the pace, the direct or indirect nature of our contributions, the constructive or destructive intention of our comments in a conversation. To make explicit and known the way a group plans to interact and the shared reasons for it can ensure the participants' deeper understanding of the nature of the exchange and a reduction in miscommunications and conflicts. In the example we are now exploring as reference, the group agreed from the very beginning that we would use a direct and honest approach to conversation; we would communicate our unfiltered thoughts with a shared understanding of that space as safe and open, but also prepared to have our words questioned and discussed. In this environment, direct and blunt critique was not seen as rude or inappropriate, but as part of a focused and intensive learning process, and therefore never brought to unresolvable situations.

Dialogue is in many ways the foundation of collectives; it is the way they decide, plan, experience, learn, know; it is as valuable to them as thinking is to an individual and as important to do it mindfully. Exercises like Design Discussions offer an opportunity to establish and support broader shared dialogues but are ultimately limited in their scope and struggle by themselves to cover entirely the dialogical dimension of collective practices, which needs to encompass varied forms of creativity and can't only be guided by defined exercises. In the context of design, dialogue can also represent the way that collectives design together and is often enriched by non-verbal contributions, sketches, prototypes, schematics, videos. Through the opportunity to express, verbally, visually, or otherwise, new meaning is added and built upon cumulatively by those participating, and even ideas and mock-ups in their most premature form act as powerful tools for co-creation, for unexpected directions. Designing through dialogue is a complementary approach to collective or transdisciplinary design practices, relying on similar attitudes towards the social dimension of work and the continuous and mutual exchange of diverse perspectives, yet not all collectives seem to be able to adopt it as easily.

Dialogue remains, in fact, a grossly overlooked approach to design practice and is often dismissed as groups fail to prioritise making time for it. Even in collective environments that are best equipped to leverage dialogue meaningfully, conversations become too often separated in either task-oriented structured exchanges or unfocused small talk that escapes the interests of the group or its purpose. If we want to help design the systems we exist within, and to actuate a process of change, of translation, that situates our fields on a more responsible and shared trajectory, it is necessary to identify dialogue as an integral part of collective design practices, not as an occasional exercise or a way to spend time but as the primary engine driving collective being and doing, a catalyst for transformative thoughts.

So it isn't simply through the introduction of periodical dedicated dialogue moments, as with Design Discussions, that this approach is fully experienced (although this could be a helpful starting point and a beneficial activity for many groups), but it includes embracing its organic use throughout the collective practice, understanding the value of spontaneous moments of conversation and making an effort to contribute to an environment that more actively provides such moments. Prolonging an after-lunch coffee, preparing a meal together, going for a walk, or spending an evening out are proactively created situations that, if used for intentional and purposeful dialogue, can expand impressively the capacity of a group, community, or collective to think and create. As a group gains experience, it also becomes easier to recognise the instances in which dialogues started during a short break from another activity become the main activity, and it is a great quality to be able as a group to acknowledge and embrace this approach, to feel open and free to be guided not by structure but by collective intention. At the risk of these suggestions coming across as awkward corporate team-building activities, in the context of a collective practice guided by collectively established aims and ideals, informal moments between individuals who have no authority over one another can serve to cultivate relations that are profound, genuine, and lasting, both personally and professionally.

It must be acknowledged however, that although embracing spontaneity sounds easy enough to try out, in a moment when working remotely has become far more common and accepted, occasions that allow for random encounters are rarer than they used to be. With slightly less socially enabling video calls, groups relying more on digital chat-based communication, and the ability to have more control over an individual's working schedule, a layer of social working culture has been lost as physical communal spaces are used less and our interactions have become less unpredictable. This is not to say that more flexible approaches to a work-life schedule are a bad thing; in fact, this collective rupture (certainly helped along by the global COVID-19 pandemic) has in many ways enabled numerous alternative ways of experiencing life, work, time, and people, some of which have merit, yet, important social elements have been lost or changed in this process. So whilst it is not very easy, or advised, to try to over-plan a spontaneous encounter, creating scenarios that could inspire unexpected directions is increasingly necessary and can't be only left to chance.

Along with some of the previously mentioned activities that collectives can adopt to favour or practise dialogue, spontaneous or planned, a collective's mechanism for self-evaluation can also base itself on the regular scheduling of group conversations. Allowing for the opportunity to have focused sessions where all members openly voice concerns, suggestions, and observations on how the collective is running can help to dissipate any building tension or unhealthy competitiveness, be a way to re-activate a sense of collectivity, and offer a space for less dominant or active voices to be heard in impactful ways. These sessions are meant to realign the collective's motivations, renovate their practice, and remain inclusive through their transformations. As with any group, a variety of interpersonal dynamics are at play, from power struggles, to sexual tension, to smaller 'cliques' forming, to biases and destructive sentiments simmering below the surface. Open dialogues help to deconstruct some of these concepts and their relation to internal power imbalances, by actively exposing and exploring them. This process can be powerful for collectives, for although conflict will always naturally occur in critically engaged communities, suspending judgement through the conscious use of dialogue, and taking the opportunity to visibilise issues, disparities, and discuss them in a non-competitive but generous, patient, and attentive way, can be enlightening and changing, even when agreeing to disagree. The very concept of agreeing to disagree is itself interesting to reflect upon, as, on the one hand, it seems to relate more to discussion rather than dialogue, where ideas are butted against each other until one is victorious or none are, while, on the other hand, the presence and visibilisation of disagreement, as described above, are often what characterise a healthy collective culture. The main distinction between the uses of this attitude in discussion or collective dialogue is in the possibilities it is meant to leave for further elaboration: in discussion being used as a conversation shutter, in dialogue as a new base to build upon.

The potential of dialogue in the management of conflict and disagreement in collective practices is also made evident by its role in decision-making processes. As we observed in earlier examples, collectives often distance themselves from processes that risk to result in the establishment of marginalised minorities, such as voting, and instead naturally and conceptually gravitate towards more discursive and inclusive methods of decision-making. While the benefits of these approaches in collective design practices don't need to be highlighted further than they already have, the discordant dynamics that more commonly keep dialogue from remaining truly collective merit a reflection. Generally speaking, there is one particularly important and frequent issue, or we could say category of issues, that markedly destabilises the inner workings of non-hierarchical structures, and that is the more or less evident consolidation of unwanted authority or leadership, a distinct portion of the collective that consciously or unconsciously exerts power over the others and breaks the balance. This can take many shapes, from the charismatic individual that floods all group conversations, to the smaller group of friends who establish their own separate aims, to the competitive individuals looking for personal recognition, to majorities that render impossible the introduction of alternative ideas. There is no singular approach to circumvent or avert this obstacle; we have observed and experienced several of them throughout our research, some of which we have already shared and others we will briefly introduce now, none of which are always useful or applicable, and not all easy to propose to a group already divided and fragmented. Some approaches may appear more childish or dull than others, but we have seen them all provide different levels of support to different groups when undertaken with commitment, effort, and a shared willingness to try.

To start with, it is important not to delay addressing problems that compromise the stability of the collective or its aims, for although it is sometimes easier to ignore issues, when there is a clearly experienced disparity, creating moments to discuss, or at the very least bring an issue to light, can be enough to see a change. Some disruptive behaviours are not always consciously so, and even if this action doesn't bring to direct results, it is likely to reinforce the awareness people have of other approaches or exercises that are attempted subsequently. When trying to ensure equal opportunities within a space of dialogue, and address the difficulty of those unable to actively contribute to an exchange, perhaps due to being overwhelmed, intimidated, or ignored by others, a few simple yet often effective actions can be attempted. Raising hands before speaking rather than jumping abruptly into a conversation can already help regulate the tendency of some to interrupt or monopolise dialogue and allow for a more clear visualisation of who is asking to speak and how often. Confident individuals that impulsively tangent into long monologues can more easily become self-aware if they see other hands raised, waiting for their turn to talk. Similarly, keeping a simple record of the main discussion points in a format that remains visible to all throughout the exchange, like on a whiteboard or a shared digital space, can ensure that ideas that have been lengthily explained and those which have only been mentioned briefly remain equally visible throughout the activity, allowing for participants to continue their reflection on them and mitigating in part the invisibilisation of ideas through the over-explanation of others. This method of record keeping is well suited to most dialogue approaches, even in experienced and socially stable groups. The practice of starting a dialogue by going around the table and asking each participant to add something to the board[3] can give everyone time to inform the context of that dialogue, the points that will be considered during the rest of the exercise, the base on which new collective knowledge will be built upon. Even visualising a vote can have powerful effects; although it is often incompatible with decision-making, voting can be a dialogue starter and a rapid tool to verify the status of the collective on a specific matter; the continued presence of contrasting votes in a visible format can prevent the forming of unspoken assumptions and guide the conversation towards more inclusive directions. In this case, voting options shouldn't be limited or geared towards the establishment of a majority, but simply aimed at indicating the diverse perspectives present in the group, so even when two positions seem to be similar enough, it is important not to group them together but instead recognise and visualise their diversity even if subtle. The whole process of writing on a shared board, of note taking, offers itself opportunities to alleviate internal tensions and increase everyone's awareness of the collective's power dynamics. It can be extremely useful to formalise and rotate a few roles that don't allow for direct engagement in conversation but instead position some members outside of the conversation, as observers, facilitators, or record keepers. If members are rotated regularly through these positions, possibly every time, the group can experience how their interactions change as some individuals become observers rather than active participants and become more conscious of each other. For those who tend to exert more power in conversations, being positioned in a role that requires attentive observation can be eye-opening; with the impossibility to talk, those individuals become more aware of their context and learn to understand the value of listening and reflecting. The practice of active listening, removed from the pressure or possibility to engage in dialogue, is a necessary step to transition from discussion to collective and creative dialogue. It is crucial to listen actively to what others are saying, to avoid occupying one's mind with the crafting of a perfect rebuttal while ignoring the surroundings, as the first thing one says is not always the most important to respond to. This also brings us to the idea of time, of pace. To practise active listening means making the time to focus on others' inputs, from beginning to end, reflecting on what has been shared before adding to it. In many cases, this may simply result in short pauses naturally occurring between one input and the next, but the time to process information is not equal to all, nor the favoured forms of communication, and longer pauses may be beneficial to maintain the collective as stimulated and engaged as possible. At times, especially when dialogues revolve around decision-making, it may be worth leaving an apparently concluded conversation for a couple of days, to then verify how the group reflections may or may not change the original outcome.

More specific to the context of design, misunderstandings present interesting opportunities for unexpected co-creation to occur, not only during the exploration of interpersonal issues but also in the act of sharing concepts and ideas throughout the design process. As we have tended towards the habit of being as explicit as possible in the way we communicate with others in design, in part for efficiency and in part thanks to improving technology, room for interpretation is decreasing and with it, the chance to understand something differently and trail off in unexpected and potentially more interesting directions. The tools and methods that we use to share ideas, from photorealistic renders to almost finished quality mock-ups, have developed towards ever-increasing levels of definition, making lesser refined options seem less relevant, less impressive, and generally more amateur, even when simply used for internal presentations. But the movement towards more technically advanced forms of concept visualisation, although impressive to some, doesn't coincide with the support of creative and collective efforts, or of dialogue. These sometimes more finalised iterations feel like a closed door, imagination is blocked by detail, the design appears more complete, and it is difficult to re-enter into a process of conceptualisation at a more abstract level. Definition forms impossibilities.

The breadth of input that a collective working environment can offer through the adoption of its members' varied skills and experiences in different modes of visualisation and conceptualisation is both valuable and dangerous. Here once again asymmetric power can be exerted by those who are more technically skilled to provide a better representation of their ideas, especially until the group remains conditioned by the superficial ways of thinking of mainstream design activity. What is needed often is a simple attitudinal change, the understanding that it is rarely the best visuals that are best for dialogue. More accessible and abstract sketches, rough plans, and fast mock-ups allow for early-stage ideas to be discussed at broader conceptual levels and result in multiple interpretations of the same thought, offering spontaneous and unexpected opportunities.

Notes

1 At the time (2016) we were third-year BA students in London and were growing frustrated with the dry and outdated curricula provided to us. We were experiencing schooling systems which were ultimately run as businesses, with the continuous cut of spaces and facilities to accommodate courses that were cheaper to run and could hold more paying students, where every square metre of their buildings was assessed on the basis of the profit it could generate

2 The participants of Design Discussions included Ruben Bendavid, Cesar Beuve-Mery, Riccardo Centazzo, Jonathan Morris, Grace Pappas, and Jaxon Pope.

3 The word 'board' is here used for simplicity, and it is not necessarily meant to refer to a physical space. Anything from a shared digital document to a piece of paper everyone is able to see could be considered under this term.

References

Bendavid, R. et al., 2016. *Design Discussions*. Available at: https://www.selcestudio. com/design-discussions (Accessed: December 10, 2022).

Bohm, D. Factor, D. and Garrett, P., 1991. *Dialogue - A Proposal*. Available at: http:// www.david-bohm.net/dialogue/dialogue_proposal.html (Accessed: October 15, 2022).

Jenlink, P.M. and Banathy, B.H., 2008. *Dialogue as a Collective Means of Design Conversation*. New York: Springer.

Sennett, R., 2013. *Together: the Rituals, Pleasures and Politics of Cooperation*. London: Penguin Books.

Vaughan, L. and Edquist, H., 2012. *Design Collective: An Approach to Practice*. Newcastle upon Tyne: Cambridge Scholars Publishing.

9 Rethinking design collectively

A pervasive feeling of inability characterises the relation that many have with the systems around them, which often appear to be inescapable, ever-present yet uncertain, systems that try to separate, categorise, quantify, and own. Their extended scale isolates more than it brings together, rendering us anxious and concerned, making us continuously doubt whether we ever have enough time, contacts, or resources to act against what is imposed on us. But if we were to offer a broad statement, based on what we have learnt reflecting on the topics of this book, towards any overwhelming sense of paralysis, it would be that nothing needs to be approached alone, because nothing is done alone.

We have been conditioned to recognise opportunities for division more than for cohesion, and we have grown specialised, defined, and detached through the over-compartmentalisation of our lives, drawing lines between work and play, private and public, one discipline and another, one person and another. However, it is between these boundaries that there appear to be possibilities, for cross-contamination, for new ways of experiencing and of understanding, for intertwining our hopes with our actions, and for moments of reciprocal exchange with unsuspecting individuals, groups, and communities.

It is unfortunate how sometimes those who develop alternative ways of thinking and practising design become convinced that they represent a rare exception, that most who work in their field don't see the issues they see, or don't think what they think. It isn't completely wrong to assume that questioning mainstream approaches through action implies being part of a minority, but it is also true that being different doesn't mean being alone. Assumptions inevitably form impossibilities, and the risk of these practices to isolate in self-referential bubbles of thought on the belief that there are no ecosystems able to support them appropriately is real and worrying. In reality, the percentage of design practitioners, researchers, students, or observers who have developed at least a basic awareness of the issues characterising their disciplines is considerable, but the distance between thought and action can feel overwhelming, and many struggle to take active steps towards a complete renovation of their practice, themselves feeling unsupported. There is a need to explore more ways to avoid distancing alternative practices from those who

DOI: 10.4324/9781003354826-10

are only a conversation away from becoming part of them and to visibilise the reciprocal need for support different groups may have in this search for different approaches.

We started this book by mentioning complexity, with the idea that the extended field of design is acknowledging both its growth and the importance of interfacing with it. Although complexity is a relative concept, it seems that most who recognise this tendency agree that there is a lack of preparation towards it, that this complexity is at a scale in which it exceeds what the field of design is, for the most part, able to engage with under the present forms of practice and organisation. Often what is suggested is the need for more collaborations between different disciplines, or for the re-evaluation of educational systems (both valid points), but not enough of these proposals try to fundamentally question the vertical structures that are perpetuating the inability to do things collectively, even though they recognise a need for it.

Complexity can't be effectively addressed individually nor through a univocal perspective. Similarly to what we have previously mentioned for contexts, their understanding happens as part of plural exchanges that are as varied as what they are aiming to uncover, as they are often mutually informing. So collective practices don't only represent a necessary and political act of inclusivity in knowledge creation but also a natural consequence of our interest, or in certain cases urgency, for dimensions of dialogue capable of interfacing with such complexity. In connecting the expert and the amateur, the researcher and the observer, the minority and the majority, the old and the young, these collective dimensions are rich but require considerable commitment and effort to manifest, needing to break down ingrained divisive approaches and instead discover alternative value systems, for example with the questioning of the relation between experience and time.

Despite the problematically common discrediting of younger generations by older ones as lazy and uninformed, we have found increasing numbers of design students and graduates in recent years displaying not only a curiosity towards the implications of their future roles in society but also a different, more reflective, and critical approach to design practice. It has become almost impossible for them to ignore the ecological and energy crisis they were born within, or to not be aware of the oppressive and discriminating nature of the realities they have experienced or observed growing up, they have had a different way to absorb reality physically and digitally, of relating to knowledge, but we don't believe this makes them uninformed or less equipped to contribute to our futures. On the contrary, it has resulted in more and more projects that question the fundamentally commercial trajectory design has been positioned on, projects about visibilising rather than producing, addressed to communities rather than consumers. We are hopeful in the future of design practice also because of what we believe younger generations are and will be able to bring to the table, with diverse ways of searching, communicating, creating, sharing, and feeling.

The myth of the older educators or practitioners being the holders of all knowledge loses traction in times of increased acceleration and change, where people born less than ten years apart are already characterised by an evidently different experience of culture and technology, and that sees 'new' knowledge becoming commonplace rapidly, at times in a matter of months. This is not to discount the value of experience, of what time can bring to one's ability to reflect and assess in both personal and professional contexts, but to suggest that there is value elsewhere too, and that if we are to engage with complex systemic questions, we need to evaluate experience not only on the basis of time but also on diversity, on complexity, that we need to avoid being exclusive of who is in a position to learn or to teach. Maybe a model such as this one will struggle finding its way through the bureaucratic nightmare educational institutions tend to be associated with, in which hierarchy is still prominent and power dynamics are kept intentionally asymmetric, but can certainly be imagined and more readily applied elsewhere, in spaces of open intersection between individuals that position knowledge sharing at the centre of a common dialogue.

We are not thinking together if we are not equally listened to; the importance of non-hierarchical, inclusive, transdisciplinary, transgenerational dimensions can't be overstated both in practice and education. If we learn to look horizontally, rather than always trying to climb vertically, in collective practices we find opportunities to be active participants in the shaping of the systems we exist within, exploring different ways to imagine and reimagine with others, to experience reciprocal generosity and more inclusive forms of knowledge creation and sharing. In their being accessible, decentralised, committed, and varied, collectives could very well represent a viable educational alternative to the unmoving, exclusive, and limiting schooling systems designers seem to be so ready to complain about but so unwilling to profoundly change. And as we see collectives developing different ways to relate to each other, either in the form of collectives of collectives, or by simply forming larger communities, a more extended educational web can form. This can be particularly relevant if we relate it to some of the observations we presented in previous chapters, if we consider any contribution or output, and therefore knowledge, as non-individual and unownable, and instead residing in the space between individuals, in the communities or contexts they are directly or indirectly contributing to, the scale of these spaces does become significant in assessing their potential.

The chance to reimagine the prevailing formats of higher education is one that should not be taken for granted; this moment in time, when collectivity as a form of organisation is becoming more understood for its value and potential across multiple disciplines, can help to radically shift the ways we think about the training that leads to a professional qualification and the concept of qualification itself. The current assessment of knowledge and experience as the sum of quantifiable elements on a résumé excludes very quickly many of the less easily described activities that sit outside of institutional or formal environments, activities that may be difficult to label as they are complex and ever-changing, or in which contributions can't rightfully be separated between individuals as they are seen as a product of the whole, such as collectives. So how will we start to assess experience under collective systems of learning? What would qualifications be based on? Will they even be necessary?

There are growing shifts in the approach towards how individuals visualise their professional and personal trajectories, their careers, what it takes to build one, if one is needed, who to know, how to act, who to become, what to care about. Not all of these trajectories separate personal and professional, the ideals one has to the actions one takes, and this can be especially true in collective practices, where the continuous questioning of boundaries and divisions results in an environment in which work, life, and learning become irreversibly entangled, where the lack of hierarchy renders job positions redundant, and the reliance on roles shifts towards a reliance on each other, a trust in one another over trust in an imposed system. With the approaches that will develop towards collectives sustaining themselves financially, logistically, emotionally, creatively, intellectually, across borders, norms, habits, and mindsets, and with disciplinary specialisations and titles starting to blur as we unceasingly intermix our perspectives and experiences. How will we begin to define ourselves? Will our titles be more based on our intentions rather than our skills? Will titles remain individual?

There are many questions that we could ask ourselves as we speculate over some of the implications collective practices may represent for our futures; it is easy to indulge in a discourse that risks slipping out of the realm of possibility and into a utopian dimension, yet, we don't think we have done so excessively or unreasonably. Throughout this book we have presented situations, observations, and ideas based on what we have interacted with and not only imagined, on realities that do exist or are not too far away from taking shape. It may seem difficult to take a step away from individually-centred systems, there are deeply rooted influences that sit in our way towards this transition, and collective practices may themselves not work for everyone, or not work every time, but it is sometimes in the experience of alternative systems that one becomes aware of their ability to explore further. If we start to participate in communities informed by values we feel represented by, able to plan and implement change, able to translate, to design, it means we are collectively connecting our critique to our actions, that we are not critical for critique's sake but because we are hopeful for what that dialogue can result in. We are, in a way, activists.

Collectives may not be the only systems that take on the challenges of an extended design field pressed by issues they don't seem to be adequately equipped for, yet we believe they will become increasingly important in pushing design's trajectory towards a more responsible and accountable path, that they will continue to push imposed boundaries and represent spaces of diversity and inclusion, of meaningful relationships and influential outcomes. They will revolutionise the idea of work to some and the idea of life to others, they will make us reflect on our plural and mutually defining identities, on the concept of friendship, solidarity, and care that has been too often streamlined away from our efficiency-focused contexts, on the meaning of time and effort, property and knowledge.

By representing non-hierarchical and dialogical dimensions, collectives reclaim open dialogue as a synonym of thinking, of learning, of creating together and challenge our perception of authorship and agency by relating to the intricate contexts we enter in contact with. They offer us ways to learn from and build on the experience of others, from collectives like projektado and their exploration of alternative forms of knowledge creation and sharing; Hay Futura, as they re-imagine the field of design through a gender perspective; ruangrupa and their daring attempts in collective organisation and education; the space of Atlantide and NullaOsta as catalysts for cultural cross-contamination; and OPAVIVARÁ! who vivaciously merge public and private.

As we reach the end of our reflections, it may seem questionable whether this book was in fact about design or not, and that is probably a good thing. In our chase for transversality and diversity in everyday practices and in our collective dimensions, talking about design, even in its most general interpretation, in isolation, seems contradictory. How can one reflect on design without reflecting on so much more? How can one sharply define a discipline without ignoring its role and position in the future? Certainly not all content can always be about everything at once; at some point we need to stop zooming out and take a moment to reflect, but also we can't contribute to divisive views of practice or knowledge. We need to see content as existing in constant overlap, not as categorisable in separate folders but as a network of communicating vessels, and we believe collectives are one of the ecosystems that allows for the transition towards this understanding.

Although this is in some ways the last chapter of our book, we have decided for it to not be a conclusion. We understand knowledge as reciprocal, as contextually informed and informing, as dynamic and transforming. There is no reason for us to strive for content that is sharply defined or self-contained, as the idea of self-containment clashes with that of transversal thinking and of collective practice. Bringing a conversation to a definite conclusion is an impossibility if we still want to hope that our ways of thinking and doing can change, if we want to start turning fixed positions into trajectories. There are many ways to contribute to a shared dialogue, we are trying to do so through this book, and we sincerely hope it will both build and be built upon as it is intertwined with the intricate network knowledge communities embody.

References

Cramer, F. and Wesseling, J., 2022. *Making Matters: A Vocabulary for Collective Arts.* Amsterdam: Valiz.

Frascara, J., 2020. *Design education, training, and the broad picture: Eight experts respond to a few questions.* The Journal of Design, Economics, and Innovation, 6(1), pp.106–117.

Illich, I., 1972. *Deschooling Society.* New York: Harper and Row.

Maldonado, T., 1970. *Design, Nature and Revolution.* United States of America: Harper & Row, Publishers, Inc.

Noël, G., 2020. *We all want high-quality design education: But what might that mean?* The Journal of Design, Economics, and Innovation, 6(1), pp.5–12.

Ockerse, T., 2012. *Learn from the core design from the core.* Visible Language, 46, pp.80–93.

Redström, J., 2020. *Certain uncertainties and the design of design education.* The Journal of Design, Economics, and Innovation, 6(1), pp.83–100.

Whiteley, N., 1993. *Design for Society.* London: Reaktion Books.

10　A directory of tools and practices

This chapter aims to collate some of the strategies and general approaches that are more commonly found in collective practices, those we have interacted with and presented for this book, as well as others we know of, situated both within and outside of design. The format, therefore, is somewhat disjointed and synthetic, as we aim to bring together a selection of useful concepts in a framework that is easier to consult and helps direct readers to the chapters (listed in order of relevance) that may more appropriately cover their topics of interest. This is in no way a comprehensive list and could certainly be built on, it is also not a list of strict guidelines or rules but rather an accessible collection of observations and reflections; designers should remain critical of the tools they adopt and be active in the development of their own ways of doing. Everyone absorbs content differently, and we hope this chapter will support different ways of experiencing and approaching our book.

Friendship/Generosity/Decentralisation

Friendship is a concept that relates to collective practices in multiple and diverse ways. It is often one of the initiating factors bringing individuals to form a group, a recurring aspect of stability for many collectives, and an inspiring social structure that can critically inform our understanding of them.

When reflected upon as a form of organisation, friendship is unique and radical. It escapes many of the pervasive logics of capitalist societies, by being a form of exchange that, on the one hand, requires effort, time, emotional commitment, and trust and, on the other hand, doesn't rely on any monetary return. They are non-hierarchical, decentralised, and lasting, established on the basis of something shared and supported by reciprocal solidarity and generosity. In representing so strikingly many of the fundamental characteristics of collectives, the concept of friendship helps to conceptualise the feasibility and value of these practices in a context obsessed with owning, reminding us of the powerful and important ways simple tools can help us disrupt and re-imagine our modes of relating to others and building new realities.

See Chapters 2, 8, 3, and 5.

DOI: 10.4324/9781003354826-11

Manifesto/Meaning/Motivation

Shared ideals, aims, and motivations are fundamental elements of cohesion in collective practices. Although they are not always made explicit, they contribute to shaping the understanding a group has of its own plural identity and can ultimately guide its outputs, suggesting the need for ways to both establish them and maintain them.

The co-creation of a manifesto between members of a collective is an activity that can stimulate rich and profound dialogue and lead to more relational understandings of oneself, each other, and the contexts the group enters into contact with. The process of collectively articulating diverse ideas and opinions, abstract or concrete, into a condensed statement, can often be more valuable than the outcome itself, acting as a catalyst towards the formation or renewal of a shared identity and the consolidation of the members' reciprocal commitment.

The manifesto itself remains a useful tool of communication for the group, in being able to describe the collective's status and visions externally and to new members and therefore shouldn't be considered impervious to change. With members coming and going, and through evolving opinions and approaches, collective practices are likely to remain dynamic and changing, and therefore the revision, re-discussion, and re-imagining of a statement of intent can ensure their position remains relevant, supporting, and inclusive.

See Chapters 3 and 4.

Dialogue/Thinking together/Learning communities

In collective practices open dialogue is the process that can most resemble that of thinking together; it is the backbone of decision-making and in many ways informs how they create. However, not all collectives manage to leverage it as effectively. The ubiquitous nature of conversation and the wide range of approaches that can be adopted within the dialogical dimension of collective practice often risk to hide or even discredit the value of more intentional, more creative dialogue.

Differently from discussion, traditionally based on the confrontation and selection of ideas, dialogue is a form of exchange (verbal, visual, physical, digital) based on open participation and the shared forming of thought. Assumptions are put aside to avoid the creation of strict boundaries, and the intention becomes to build on each other's ideas rather than to oppose unmovable opinions until one is chosen. Participants are not preoccupied with changing others to conform to their own vision but to see ideas as naturally transforming and evolving. What is talked about is understood as a product of that moment, not of individual participants, a thought that is always collective because it is enabled by the impossibly intricate entanglement of inputs, ideas, feelings, and ways of knowing that establishes the context in which those thoughts are formed and shared.

Dialogue further reinforces collectives as highly effective learning communities and as spaces of shared authorship and knowledge, of generosity. However, it is not always easy to maintain dialogue inclusive, balanced, or relevant, and at times it may be hard to initiate it in the first place. A number of approaches and exercises can be adopted to favour the continuation of meaningful dialogues, from the practice of active listening, to the visibilisation of disparities.

See Chapters 8, 4, 3, 5, 7, and 9.

Decision-making/Conflict/Power

In a non-hierarchical collective situation where everyone has equal say and responsibility, ensuring the approach to making decisions continuously supports the fundamental values of collective being is critical and at times complex. There are a number of different methods that can be effectively employed, depending on the group, its size, its internal dynamics, or its context, yet there seems to be some recurring elements that often characterise these collective processes.

One is the need for everyone to be represented by the choices the collective makes, meaning that everyone should have equal opportunities to influence said choices. This is often maintained through a policy of decision-making based on consensus and consensus building and therefore on the intensive use of dialogue as an enabler for the creation of shared understandings and knowledge. Compared to other methods, consensus through dialogue can increase the time it takes for shared ideas to be established, decisions to be made, and plans to move to action. Some may find this approach frustrating, especially when experiencing for the first time how it differs from the options used in more vertical and efficiency-oriented structures, but time is a factor people have to learn to establish a different relation to when in collectives, if they truly want to explore and experience an alternative dimension of practice. If approached with commitment, effort, openness, and willingness to support the continuation of a shared collective ecosystem, dialogue can provide a way to make decisions as well as to resolve conflict, to address the ever-present concern for power imbalances, and to keep the group inclusive and diverse.

At first glance, voting may appear to solve some of the aforementioned issues, like that of time or the resolution of complex situations or conflicts, yet there are reasons for many collectives to not naturally gravitate towards this method. Voting by majority means making choices that don't represent all equally but one group over others. While in certain contexts this may be less problematic, in collective practices the invisibilisation of some members through practices that fail to represent them creates deep fractures, endangers diversity, and pushes unacknowledged members further away from both the outputs of their collective and its identity.

See Chapters 8, 4, 3, 5, 2, and 6.

Scale/Reach/Complexity

Scale plays a fundamental role in the organisation and complexity of a collective practice, from methods of communication, to decision-making and conflict resolution processes, from the diverse range of perspectives present in the group, to the time required to think together. Being a very contextually dependent concept, the influence of scale shouldn't be discussed in absolutes, and it is more easily observed through the experience of a collective growing or decreasing in numbers. Pace, complexity, and reach are three commonly noted factors in these transitions.

With fewer members, collectives can often increase the pace of decision-making processes, as organisation overall may appear more manageable and efficient, but a lack of complexity also leads to a more limited capacity to remain relevant over time, in the higher chance of stagnating thoughts, and a less rich, varied, and transforming practice. There are several methods smaller collectives can employ to make up for this limit, including inviting guests to meetings or group discussions, initiating external collaborations, approaching other collectives to exchange experiences, embarking on projects of greater complexity that require interaction with outside actors, and more.

With growing numbers, collectives can have access to more interconnected and wider networks, an extended reach that, depending on their context, may establish a group as a significant force in their fields or their communities. Internal power dynamics become increasingly more complex; the maintenance of a non-hierarchical system and of a collective identity that all feel equally represented by requires more attention and time, as all forms of organisation tend to do as well. In their need for more frequent maintenance processes, larger groups are naturally more dynamic and positively unstable, leveraging difference to produce more informed knowledge. With a greater amount of variables at play, the balance between too little structure and too much is ever present, at times resulting in interpersonal bonds losing depth, and sometimes even to transitions towards completely different organisational structures.

See Chapters 4, 3, 5, and 8.

Transdisciplinarity/Cross-contamination/Difference

Embracing transversality and cross-contamination is both crucial for design collectives intentioned to have an output that is complex and important and a necessary way to envision design practice in a less divisive future.

The sustained interaction between diverse backgrounds in a collective and non-hierarchical environment opens the opportunity for a dialogue that isn't just reciprocally informing but also co-forming, creative. By becoming less conditioned by sectoral boundaries and gaining unexpected perspectives, the role of each discipline is re-understood in its relation to others, breaking down the isolating bubbles of knowledge and action that have for long been constructed and redistributing responsibilities and purposes. Through this approach the idea of 'expert' is questioned and challenged and that of knowledge communities reinforced.

Complexity is better grasped by groups than by individuals, and when those groups are themselves holders of complex knowledge, the learning path for those involved becomes more direct and continuously motivating, pushing them forward together in their shared willingness to translate and change. For designers, this results in the participation in projects of broader scope, in the interaction with the systems of living and thinking that shape our current and possibly future dimensions.

See Chapters 1, 3, 5, 4, 9, 8, and 7.

Visibilising effort/Rotation of tasks/Awareness

The value of some roles or contributions over others can be at times difficult to grasp in a collective. Certainly there are opportunities to share responsibility quite effectively over specific tasks, and the presence of a common vision can facilitate the understanding of all contributions as necessary, but often certain activities appear more evidently than others and not everyone's work is equally acknowledged. Sometimes this is an accidental result of faulted group dynamics, other times egos still make their appearance in ecosystems that are supposed to be shared.

The invisibilisation of effort can be a serious issue in the internal balance of collective practices and one that can risk pushing members to the margins or outside of the group if not addressed. Less tangible actions can be actively made visible sometimes by simply acknowledging them in a collective context, by thanking those responsible for them, or by making their insights more present in open conversations.

A more effective method to favour a more distributed awareness of the collective's practice is that of periodically rotating roles or tasks. Depending on the collective, time availability, and the complexity of tasks and projects, this action can be more or less difficult to arrange, but it has the potential to be quite powerful. Through this approach members enter in a process of collective learning and teaching, redefining bonds and understandings between members, and producing more consistently unexpected and creative ways to undertake tasks.

See Chapters 8, 7, 4, and 5.

Authorship/Identity/Plurality

In societies and fields of work more actively supporting the concepts of individual recognition and ownership, the adoption of a shared identity is a radical and political statement. The way that collectives handle their common identity and signature is critical to the external perception of the group and to the internal understandings of how and why something is created and shared. Many collectives decide to sign their work as a group, under one commonly established name, which both represents and informs a culture where decentralisation, inclusivity, plurality, transversality, generosity, and sharing are values that become prioritised, enacted, and made sustainable. Through this action and the distributed approach to authorship, members also relate to responsibility differently, feeling accountable not only for their own designated tasks or roles (if the collective distributes as such) but also for the work of their peers, which gives space for a less competitive and more mutually sustaining ecosystem, where members fundamentally learn to care and trust each other as a part of practice.

In a further step away from the self-serving and self-centred actions that characterise vertical structures and the contemporary culture of visibility, some collectives choose to keep their members' individual identities hidden or non-explicit. Anonymisation can be both a powerful and dangerous tool for a collective, risking on one side to invisibilise some of the underlying dimensions of a complex practice but simultaneously providing an additional layer of meaning to what it may signify to see oneself as part of something guided by shared goals and ideals rather than individual ones.

Questioning the prevailing ideas of identity and authorship is a necessary step to form alternative understandings of how knowledge is created and how different practices contribute to their contexts.

See Chapters 6, 7, 3, 4, 5, and 2.

Context/Contact/Contribution

Through the use of dialogue, of shared identity and authorship, and the understanding of a collective's output as the manifestation of a specific situation, of the reciprocal contacts that give shape to a collective, rather than a simple sum of the members' inputs, we are brought to question both the plausibility of original and completely individual ideas and the very idea of contribution.

Most of the time contextual, environmental, or sensorial factors have as much influence on the result of a conversation as the direct participation of someone might, the presence or absence of someone, the layout of a space, the weather outside, the socio-cultural dimension of that encounter are all elements that actively or passively shape the collective's process of thinking and producing; they are all contributors. Under this light, authorial attribution becomes more complex, now not only equally shared between a group of people but perhaps also with a much more extended network of contributing factors and situations, a context as designer.

This perspective can help collectives to recognise the importance of maintaining a stimulating and motivating context, of extending and varying, of entering in contact with increasingly complex elements. It helps to give a different value to contributions, understand the lack of something to be as influential as its presence, preparing a meal as powerful as presenting an idea. It helps recognising commitment and participation in ways more compatible with the idea of collective being and debunking the concept of ownership of knowledge.

See Chapters 7, 8, 9, 5, 4, 3, and 6.

Hope/Critique/Action

Hope is a powerful underlying force in the imagining and re-imagining of our contexts, of our knowledge, and ourselves. It sustains the continuation of creative endeavours, the fundamental idea of generosity and friendship, of solidarity, of care and activism. Whether or not the ideals and aims that guide a collective are considered to be radical or revolutionary, the exploration of alternative ways of doing is often fuelled by the belief that change can be brought to a situation of interest.

While being critical is often the first step towards enacting change, hope is a necessary requirement to translate critique to action, and environments that facilitate the establishment of hopeful aims can more easily support this transformative movement.

Although we could see design as a naturally hopeful practice (at times blindly so), as it is based on the planning and implementation of change and the expectation that our actions will make some difference to someone, when looking at the field of design practice and the prevailing schooling/working systems developed around it, it is quite common to see critique deprived of action, or action not informed by critique, and a general loss of connection between responsible reflection and the world it is supposed to help inform and transform.

Collectives are instead intrinsically hopeful structures for the simple fact that they invest effort in questioning much of what constitutes their surrounding realities. They propose models of learning, thinking, and creating that inspire change and models of living and being that take apart and reconstruct our everyday life in unexpected ways. A collective practice interested in design processes amplifies this approach, constructs shared visions based on the entanglement of diverse thoughts, on the transversal understanding of practice, and the reciprocal nature of responsibility, and more actively establishes implementing paths for their collective aims.

See Chapters 9, 3, 4, and 5.

Index